POLITICS AND PERSONALITIES

POLITICS AND PERSONALITIES

With Other Essays by

THE RIGHT HON.
GEORGE W. E. RUSSELL

Essay Index Reprint Series

BOOKS FOR LIBRARIES PRESS, INC.
FREEPORT, NEW YORK

First Published 1917
Reprinted 1967

LIBRARY OF CONGRESS CATALOG CARD NUMBER: 67-26778

PRINTED IN THE UNITED STATES OF AMERICA

TO

LANCELOT RIDLEY PHELPS

PROVOST OF ORIEL

IN HONOUR OF A FRIENDSHIP

WHICH BEGAN WHEN WE WERE FRESHMEN

NOTE

THIS book owes its existence to the kindness of Mr. Fisher Unwin, who happened to see some of the papers which compose it, and judged them worthy of reproduction.

My best thanks for permission to reproduce them are due to the Editors of the *Daily News*, the *Manchester Guardian*, the *Nation*, and the *Cornhill Magazine*.

G. W. E. R.

June 26, 1917.

CONTENTS

I.—POLITICS AND THE CONSTITUTION

II.—IDEALS AND WAR

9

CONTENTS

III.—PERSONALITIES, ANCIENT AND MODERN

IV.—MISCELLANEA

CONTENTS

I

POLITICS AND THE CONSTITUTION

I

TYRANNICIDE

I WAS lately addressing an audience of working men on the ethical aspects of war. After the address there was a discussion, and the question which excited the keenest debate was : " What are we to do with the Kaiser when the war is over? " In vain I reminded my friends of the adage about catching your hare before you cook him. Some—a few—were for St. Helena ; the great majority were for capital punishment —either by shooting, as befits an officer and a gentleman, or by hanging, as the appropriate doom of one who has placed himself outside the pale of humanity. These interesting dissertations turned my thoughts to the venerable theme of Tyrannicide—to those who have practised it, and to those others who, in prose or in verse, have extolled it.

One of the strangest incidents in Lord

Beaconsfield's strange career was his *Revolutionary Epick*. It was his first and last venture in poetry, and was published in 1834, with an amazing preface :—

Standing upon Asia and gazing upon Europe, with the broad Hellespont alone between us, and the shadow of Night descending on the mountains, these mighty continents appeared to me as it were the Rival Principles of Government that at present contend for the mastery of the world. What ! I exclaimed, is the Revolution of France a less important event than the Siege of Troy ? Is Napoleon a less interesting character than Achilles ? For me remains the Revolutionary Epick.

He accepted the task thus magnificently suggested, but discharged it with such indifferent success that the book fell flat, and the disgusted author, to use his own quaint phrase, " hurled his lyre to Limbo." But of this unappreciated *Epick* a few lines survived, and were reproduced, to their author's consternation, thirty years later :—

Pharaoh's doom
Shall cool those chariot-wheels now hot with blood ;
And blessed be the hand that dares to wield
The regicidal steel that shall redeem
A nation's sorrow with a tyrant's blood.

TYRANNICIDE

In the session of 1864 John Bright, extenuating the charge of incitement to Tyrannicide which had been brought against Mazzini, referred to this remarkable passage ; but, unfortunately, he had not armed himself with the quotation, and Disraeli promptly disavowed it ; but he qualified the disavowal by publishing, after a decent interval, a new edition of the *Epick,* in which this passage about the regicidal steel and the tyrant's blood was discreetly watered down. Some tiresome investigator — I think Mr. T. P. O'Connor—detected the alteration, and A. M. Sullivan made effective use of the unaltered passage in defending the German Socialist, Johann Most, who was charged in 1881 with inciting to the murder of European sovereigns.

Like all good Whigs, I revere the sacred year 1688, and among the many blessings which it has brought us is a singular immunity from Royal tragedies. Shakespeare, poor man, had only the materials of a ruder age out of which to construct his historical dramas. Could he have lived to see the beneficent reign of Whiggery he would have put something more ' cheerful into Richard's mouth than those dismal lines about the deaths of kings :—

How some have been deposed ; some slain in war ;
Some haunted by the ghosts they have deposed ;
Some poisoned by their wives ; some sleeping kill'd ;
All murder'd.

For murder he would have shown a more excellent way. He would have described the nocturnal flight of James II from Whitehall, by the horse-ferry at Lambeth, to the Old Kent Road, and so to the coast and to hospitable France. He would have dwelt with picturesque emphasis on the fatal act of dropping the Great Seal into the Thames (which constitutional pedants called an act of abdication), and would have shown the world that regicide is not the only method by which an irritated nation can change a dynasty.

Macaulay said : " In all honest and re-flecting minds there is a conviction, daily strengthened by experience, that the means of effecting every improvement which the Constitution requires may be found within the Constitution itself." Macaulay, as we all know, had his heightened and emphatic way of saying things, but in this passage he saves himself from the peril of over-statement by the judicious use of "honest and reflecting." There were movements, both in the eighteenth and in the nineteenth century, which seemed to challenge the capacity of the Constitution to effect all needful changes; but Macaulay would have said that the minds which directed those movements were neither "honest" nor "reflecting." Certainly the Cato Street Conspiracy of 1820, which aimed at establishing a Republic, and hoped to attract popular sympathy by parading the streets with the heads of the Cabinet Ministers borne on poles, showed little honesty and less reflection. The conspiracy failed, as it deserved to fail; and, though the half-suppressed murmur of revolutionary voices was heard, on and off, during the next

19

ten years, the auspicious event of June 20, 1837, effectually hushed them. But it is not always remembered that, again and again tragedy in its blackest form came very near the young Queen's path. To the end of her long life she could never drive down Constitution Hill without a shuddering recollection of the attempt made on that spot, within six months of her marriage, to murder herself and her husband; and on a similar attempt in 1849 Lord Shaftesbury wrote in his diary: " The profligate George IV passed through a life of selfishness and sin without a single proved attempt to take it. This mild and virtuous young woman has four times already been exposed to imminent peril."

That is the fact; and it is significant. The horrible tragedies of Royalty, so mercifully averted in England and so sadly realized in other countries, do not usually fall under the category of Tyrannicide. No one who heard it can ever forget the organ-voice of pathetic indignation in which Gladstone, on the assassination of the Czar who had emancipated the serfs, declaimed the majestic lines :—

> Let tyrants govern with an iron rod ;
> Oppress, destroy, and be the scourge of God ;
> Since he, who like a father held his reign—
> So soon forgot—was just and mild in vain.

When Abraham Lincoln fell, shot through the head, in the theatre at Washington, the assassin sprang on to the stage, exclaiming, " Sic semper tyrannis ! " and the strange inaptness of the phrase threw a new light upon political assassination. Carnot and Garfield and McKinley are names that tell the same tale ; and, nearer home, the assassins of the Phœnix Park butchered an eminently humane administrator, and with him an English stranger who had not an enemy in the world.

The " regicidal steel " may inspire the excited authors of *Revolutionary Epicks,* and Charlotte Corday may have her rightful place in the Kalendar of Humanitarianism ; but, before we can justify Tyrannicide

21

we must be sure that we have found a
Tyrant, and tyrants do not readily emerge
from the well-ordered freedom of the modern
world.

II

A FORGOTTEN PHRASE

" PEACE, Retrenchment, and Reform." These
words carry us back to the first quarter
of the nineteenth century. They formulate
the desire of a people exhausted by the
French War, taxed to bursting-point, and
scandalously misgoverned. Peace was the
ideal of the humanitarians and philosophers ;
Reform the ideal of the politicians ; and,
between the two, the economists, speaking
by the mouth of Joseph Hume, inserted
Retrenchment of a profligate and crushing
expenditure.

The phrase hit the popular fancy, and
it held its own as an epitome of Liberal
aspirations for thirty years after the Reform
Bill had become law. But gradually the
old ideals lost their attractiveness, and new
theories of national prosperity made them-

selves heard. To Matthew Arnold, surveying English politics with the dispassionate
gaze of the critical outsider, the sacred
formula seemed nothing but the " creed
outworn " of a comfort-worshipping Philis-
tinism, destitute of intelligence and ideas ;
and he suggested as an amendment and
expansion of it—" Peace to our nonsense,
Retrenchment of our profligate expenditure
of claptrap, and Reform of ourselves."

This counsel, given first in 1866, seemed
harsh and unpalatable to young and ardent
Liberals, just delivered from Palmerston's
paralysing influence and rejoicing in the
imminent triumph of democracy. To be
told, and told by a writer on the Liberal
side, that our political philosophy was
nonsense, that our eloquence was claptrap,
and that we had better try to reform
ourselves before we attempted to right the
world, was a painful experience ; but we
refused to be daunted. We pinned our
faith upon Bright and Gladstone, and we
honestly believed that, if only the artisans
could get the vote, we should soon see

a new heaven and a new earth. For a
while our faith seemed to be justified.
The artisans came into their kingdom in
1868, and for the next five years we
saw, at any rate, some approximation to
the triumph of our principles. The democracy made Gladstone Prime Minister; and,
whatever else he did or failed to do, he
kept England at peace when Europe was
drenched in blood and the United States
were clamouring for redress; he retrenched
expenditure with an even meticulous care;
and he effected some reforms which touched
the bases of national life. The administration of 1868-74 left its permanent mark
on our politics, and the Imperialist reaction under Lord Beaconsfield was a protest
against the policy which had " shaken the
citadel of privilege to its base." Gladstone's
later administrations added very little to
his earlier achievements; and, as the Glad-
stonian spirit subsided, the reaction, which
had begun under Lord Beaconsfield, extended
itself, at first insensibly, to the Liberal
Party.

It would be invidious to indicate the personal channels through which this poison
of Imperialism made its way into the body
of the Liberal Party. What is noteworthy,
and lamentable, is that a pernicious influence, communicated from above, found a
ready lodgment in the very class to which
reformers had looked for a resolute maintenance of the old ideals. For twenty
years the Liberal Party, sterilized and impotent, saw its watchwords scouted ; and
its appointed work performed, if performed
at all, by its political opponents. The
General Election of 1906 gave promise of
better things. As a Party-triumph it was
complete, but the victory had been won on
an economic issue. The constituencies had
been stirred into unusual activity by the
menace of " Tariff Reform." They would
have nothing to do with what Lord Goschen
aptly called " a gamble in the food of the
people " ; and, if only a candidate was
sound on that immediate and most practical issue, his sentiments on other questions, equally fundamental but less urgent,
26

were not taken into account. Sir Henry
Campbell-Bannerman was a staunch adherent
of the old watchwords ; but, when Mr.
Balfour suddenly resigned, circumstances
forced " C.-B." to take into his administration a good many men whose opinions
about Peace and Retrenchment differed
widely from his own. The Prime Minister
and all his colleagues, whether " Imperial-
ists " or " Little Englanders," were reformers, and we have reaped, and are still
reaping, the fruits of their reforming zeal.
But some of them had contracted the in-
fection of militarism, and had justified the
carnage and rapine of South Africa. War
and Retrenchment are incompatible ideals,
and so two words of the vital three have
gradually slipped out of the Party-motto.

But war is not the only form of outlay
against which it behoves the advocates of
Retrenchment to protest. Every six months
sees the birth of some new Board or
Department or Commission or Committee ;
each of these institutions creates a large
array of chairmen, secretaries, clerks, and

inspectors; and these good men, though no doubt they love their country, have no notion of serving it for naught. The proposed nationalization of the Liquor-Traffic would mean the formation of a new and vast army of Civil Servants, with a Minister of State at its head. For my own part, I hate being governed and inspected and examined; and when I feel that I have to pay (even in part) the spectacled gentleman in seedy black who calls on behalf of the Inland Revenue, or the pert youth in blue serge and brown boots who wants to know if my kitchen-maid is insured, I long to lead an insurrection against our new bureaucracy.

When we look from the lower to the higher ranks of these expensive tyrannies, I seem, not seldom, to perceive the taint of political jobbery—"My agent is a capital fellow—very keen for the Unionist Party, but not too scrupulous. He very nearly got me into a scrape last time. Couldn't you make him a Commissioner of something?" "Mr. Chadband's chapel is

28

a centre of Liberal activity in my division. He has a very clever daughter, who would make a capital Inspector." But, after all, we are only living again the experiences of triumphant Liberalism under Grey and Melbourne and Althorp and the great men of 1830-41. Sydney Smith, who had fought for Peace, Retrenchment, and Reform when the cause was unpopular, smiled at the sequel of the victory when he saw Melbourne at the head of the administration—

Strange and ludicrous are the changes in human affairs. The Tories are now on the treadmill, and the well-paid Whigs are riding in chariots, with many faces, however, looking out of the windows (including that of our Prime Minister) which I never remember to have seen in the days of the poverty and depression of Whiggism. Liberalism is now a lucrative business. Whoever has any institution to destroy may consider himself as a Commissioner and his fortune as made. . . . The whole earth is in commission, and the human race, saved from the flood, is delivered over to barristers of six years' standing. The burden of proof now lies upon any man who says he is not a Commissioner ; the only doubt on seeing a new man among the Whigs is, not whether he is a Commissioner or not, but whether it is of Tithes, Poor

29

Laws, Boundaries of Boroughs, Church Leases, Charities, or any of the thousand human concerns which are now worked by Commissioners to the infinite comfort and satisfaction of mankind.

Change the titles of these offices for their modern equivalents, and you have a fair picture of triumphant bureaucracy in these latter days.

III

ARISTOCRACY

INTERPRETATION by etymology is always
precarious. Long ago the acute Whately
illustrated this truth by the instance of
the Sycophant, who, etymologically, was
a discoverer of figs, but in real life is a
toady. Cowper contemned—

> The works of learn'd philologists, who chase
> A panting syllable through Time and Space ;
> Start it at home, and hunt it in the dark,
> To Gaul, to Greece, and into Noah's ark.

Yet the study of words has its uses ;
and as we follow " Aristocracy," through
Thucydides, Plato, and Aristotle, from its
first meaning—the Rule of the Best-born
—till it comes to signify " the Rule of

the Best," we trace a certain development
of human reason. To live under the rule
of the Best-born is an ignominy which
even so staunch a lover of the ancient
ways as Edmund Burke repudiated. Of
Aristocracy in this sense he said : " If the
Constitution must perish, I would rather
by far see it resolved into any other form
than lost in that austere and insolent domination." But to live under the Rule
of the Best has been, time out of mind,
the ambition of such as frame Utopias.
Generally, they have been agreed with Sir
Thomas More that the most certain way
of choosing the Best is by popular election, and modern propagators of Utopian
ideas have formulated their doctrine in some
such words as these : " Away with the
spirit of Party-! Bring the battle of kites
and crows to an end. Let the nation,
either directly or through a representative
apparatus, choose thirty, or forty of its
best men to fill the chief offices of State ;
and, that done, let it surrender all government into the chosen hands, knowing that

nothing and nobody can improve on the Best."

To this prescription an ordinary Englishman, whatever his political convictions, is apt to reply : " Not so. Even the best is liable to corruption, and nothing is so certain to corrupt an administration as the knowledge that it holds a blank cheque, and can draw without restraint on the confidence and support of the State." It was because Gladstone had been all but deified by the General Election of 1880 that the Liberal Government entered on its mad career in Egypt, Ireland, and the Soudan. It was because Lord Salisbury could count on the support of both sides that the South African War was possible. When, as in 1906, a Liberal Government has such a vast majority that it can despise the Irish vote, it drops the question of Home Rule, and only picks it up again when a diminished majority gives scope for effective criticism. Even a Ministry of All the Talents and All the Virtues, such as that under which we just now have

C   33

the happiness to live, will probably do its work all the better because the Irish leaders have stayed, outside and can speak their mind when alike independent Liberalism and Conservative opposition have been muzzled.

So much for that abnegation of criticism, which dwellers in Utopia recommended; but there is an antecedent, and a still graver, difficulty. How can your forty Best Men be brought to act together, when, with motives equally patriotic, they are sharply divided by their rival theories of the public good? In normal times, the answer is that it is impossible. Authority and Freedom—Privilege and Equality—Collectivism and Individualism—Free Exchanges and Close Monopolies—these ideas, and a dozen others which might be cited, may in theory be not absolutely incompatible; but, in practice, realities are stronger than words, and principles, even when not verbally expressed, have a way of making themselves felt in action.

This is the reason why in normal times

34

a Government of the Best is only an Utopian dream. But we are living in a time not normal. Since August 1914 the face of the political world has been made new. The questions which then separated one Englishman from another have fallen into a very distant background ; and the State has no difficulty in finding its forty Best Men of one mind with regard to the supreme issue of the moment. Those who have been trained in the traditions of English public life do not love Coalitions ; but, if the Cabinet as now reconstituted really contains the most serviceable brains and calmest nerves and highest characters which Parliament can supply, then I wish it God-speed with all my heart, and every patriot will say Amen.[1]

An absolute unity of mind and purpose among men of otherwise conflicting sentiments is possible where a' great principle emerges, and dominates all secondary issues. To-day such a principle animates us all, and

[1] Mr. Asquith reconstituted his administration in May 1915.

it is the serious conviction that our one duty as a State is to crush the militarism of Germany. As far as that principle is concerned, there is no more likelihood that Englishmen will differ than that the sun will fail in the heavens, or the hills will melt. The risk lies in another quarter, and it is the part of good citizenship to guard against it. No difference will arise about the principle of our national action : the end which we all seek is one. But there is a possibility of difference about methods, and a frightful responsibility will rest on any one—politician, journalist, or colonial bishop [1]—who endeavours to create a schism in the Government and in Parliament over the question of compulsory service. As Mr. Asquith said the other day, a truce between parties for the period of the war, and even close association for Imperial purposes, does not mean that we have abandoned our ideals.

It must be remembered that the danger

[1] One of the South African Bishops was making "Jingo" speeches at this time.

36

of attack from without, and the defence-
less condition of our shores, were never
the true motives of the cry for Conscription.
The true motive was political and anti-
democratic. If you take an English lad
from his home, his friends, his chosen
avocation ; deprive him of his natural
freedom ; and force him through the mangle
of a barrack and a regiment ; you have, no
doubt, taught him, unless his nature be
exceptionally robust, the lesson of obedience—of submission to an authority which
he has not helped to create ; of willingness
to surrender his private judgment to commands which he does not understand. In
fine, you have done all you can to extinguish the virtues of self-governing citizenship,
and have laid, so far as is in your power,
the foundation of 'an insolent despotism.
This, I believe, is the ideal of Empire,
as it presents itself to the minds of our
military and literary and episcopal con-
scriptionists. Swinburne, who read the
thoughts of those false prophets as clearly
as Mr. Sargent reads the characters of

his sitters, put the creed of Jingoism into
ringing verse :—

> But we know, we believe it, we see it—
> Force only has power upon earth—

and he gave us our reply :—

> So be it ! and ever so be it
> For souls that are bestial by birth !

IV

THE HAWARDEN KITE

IT is exactly thirty years since the remarkable creature whose name stands at the head of this paper began its eventful flight.[1] For that name I have Lord Morley's high authority; but, as some of my readers may have forgotten it, and others may never have heard it, I will treat it historically.

The General Election of 1885 was just over. The Liberal Party had gone into the election pledged up to the eyes against Home Rule, and, though Gladstone had been secretly converted to it, his conversion was known only to a privileged few. The election had resulted in a tie. The Tories had been in office since the previous June. The Irish members were then acting

[1] Written in December 1915.

with the Tories, and the Liberals were just too few to defeat the combination. Lord Salisbury and his colleagues, therefore, retained office, but it was obvious that the life of their Administration hung on a thread.

As soon as the results of the election were complete, a little knot of active Radicals assembled under the late Mr. Chamberlain's hospitable roof at Highbury, to discuss the Parliamentary situation thus created. Very soon the sentiments of this conclave began to ooze out; and, if correctly reported, they amounted to a repudiation of Gladstone's leadership. Gladstone and Chamberlain had fought the election in complete independence of one another, and Chamberlain had no wish to see his former chief replaced in command. The policy of Highbury was to leave the Tories in office, and press them into measures of domestic reform, such as Chamberlain had proposed in his "unauthorized programme," and Gladstone had ignored.

Now there was in those days a busy

journalist called Wemyss Reid, who edited the *Leeds Mercury,* and there was a zealous M.P. called Herbert Gladstone (now Lord Gladstone), who sat for Leeds. Nothing could be more natural than that these two should discuss the rumours of what had happened at Highbury. If the plot against Gladstone's authority was to be defeated, it must be by some bold stroke which would rally Liberal opinion to Gladstone's side. An earnest but maladroit attempt to deal this stroke was made by the Leeds M.P. in conversation with the Leeds Editor, and the manager of a Press Agency was called into council.

" Unluckily," says Lord Morley, " it would seem to need at least the genius of a Bismarck to perform the delicate office of inspiring a modern oracle on the journalistic tripod." There never was anything Bismarckian about Lord Gladstone, who simply told his own opinions about his father's attitude towards Home Rule, and left his journalistic friends to use the information as they thought best for the Liberal cause. The result

was that in a communication from the
National Press Agency on the night of
December 16, and in the *Standard* and
the *Leeds Mercury* of December 17, it
was announced that Mr. Gladstone, if
returned to power, was prepared to deal in
a liberal spirit with the demand for Home
Rule.

Even after the lapse of thirty years I
can feel the shock of that announcement.
No Zeppelin has ever dropped a more
startling or more disastrous bomb than that
which fell from the " Hawarden Kite."
Down to December 1885, English politicians who were favourable to Home Rule,
or, indeed, had seriously considered it, might
be counted on the fingers of one hand.
Denunciations of Parnell's aims and methods
had been the commonplaces of Liberal,
as well as Conservative, oratory. In some
districts the Liberals had won by defying
the Irish vote, and swearing hostility to
Home Rule. This, for example, was the
case of Sir Henry James (afterwards Lord
James of Hereford) at Bury. " Mr. Glad-

stone," he said, " has been more than a leader to me—he has been a father. But, even if he were to go down on his knees, and beg me to vote for Home Rule, I should be constrained by conscience to say him Nay."

Suddenly the Liberal party was called to approve what it had hitherto been taught to condemn, and no one knew for certain on what authority the call was made. On the 17th of December Gladstone told the world by telegraph that the statement in the papers was not an accurate representation of his views, but a speculation upon them ; and that it had been published without his knowledge or authority. Lord Morley has justly observed that the publication was neither to Gladstone's advantage, nor consistent with his political strategy. " Never was there a moment when every consideration of political prudence more imperatively counselled silence." But the silence was broken beyond repair ; the Kite had mounted, and the bomb had fallen.

The explosion was followed by a storm
of questions, contradictions, explanations,
enthusiasms, and jeremiads. But amidst
all the hurly-burly Gladstone held his peace.
He would neither confirm nor deny. The
public must wait and see. The subject
was one which could only be handled by
a responsible Ministry. The intriguers, the
quidnuncs, and the busybodies had the time
of their lives. They ran hither and thither
seeking information, finding none but in-
venting much, cross-questioning politicians
and wire-pulling the Press. To one of
this enquiring tribe Gladstone wrote on the
23rd of December—

Of the conditions of any measure for Ireland, or
of my own intentions about one, I have not given to
any human being any binding indication : beyond
this, that if the Government take up the question, my
desire is to give them the best aid that, with a
reasonable freedom of judgment, I may.

The bewilderment and confusion of the
Liberal Party were absolute. No one knew
what was coming next ; who was on which
side ; or whither his party—or, indeed, him-

self—was tending. For politicians, it was a troublous Christmas. By February 1886 Gladstone was again Prime Minister, pledged to Home Rule in a form scarcely distinguishable from separation. Six strenuous months followed. The Liberal Party was rent asunder. The Home Rule Bill was thrown out. Another General Election took place. By August 1886 the constituencies had rejected Gladstone's Irish policy, and the Tories had entered on a lease of power which lasted till the end of 1905. Such is the history of the " Hawarden Kite." After thirty years' gyrations, it seems to be settling down ; though I understand that, just for the moment, it is suspended in mid-air.

V

JOHN BULL IN IRELAND

As a rule, I am wholly free from the
dramatic illusion. To me a play is a
performance, good or bad as the case
may be, but bearing little or no relation
to reality. An exception to this rule was
supplied by " John Bull's Other Island."
When the Liberal Carpet-bagger proclaimed
to the Irish peasants the immortal truth
that " What Ireland wants is a strong
Liberal Government," my own voice came
back to me, echoed from the platform
of the 'eighties. John Bull in Ireland
is not seen at his best ; but, before we
discuss his doings, let us consider his
character.

In the first place, we are no longer,
as Ruskin used to say that we were, " undegenerate in race—a race mingled of the
46

best northern blood." Within the last fifty years abundant tributaries of foreign blood —French, German, Jewish, American—have flowed into the main life-current of the nation. Even I who pen these pages, though a thorough-going Briton, am not of purely English blood. I am compounded of English and Celtic blood in the proportion of two and two. And, whenever the Celtic element is introduced, it modifies even visibly the phlegmatic temperament which used to characterize John Bull.

Then, again, as to his external characteristics, the type has changed out of all recognition, as every one can see who compares a snapshot of a contemporary crowd with *Punch's* John Bull of fifty years ago. When the external characteristics are completely changed, do the internal characteristics remain what they were? In some respects, yes. Burke professed his reliance on " the ancient and inbred integrity and piety, good nature and good humour of the English people " ;

47

and those qualities are still the bed-rock of national character. In spite of all that is said, England remains the most religious country in Europe. I am old enough to remember the astonishment of the French newspapers when, at the crisis of King Edward's dangerous illness of 1871, the English people betook themselves, like one man, to prayer. And the phenomenon which then caused so much astonishment is a commonplace to-day.

But while this characteristic of essential religiousness remains the same, it certainly has gathered round it, of late years, some less admirable attributes. The old John Bull was obstinate, pig-headed, narrow-minded ; but he was not hypocritical— or rather, his was an inverted hypocrisy. He was ashamed of seeming as good as he really was, and was apt to keep his spiritual experiences to himself. Quite different is the aspect which he presents to a critical world to-day. Here is an American appreciation of him : " The Briton is the modern Pharisee, who has looted

48

the world, and for a pretence makes long prayers. He never ceases to boast that he whipped France at Waterloo and Trafalgar, and bested the whole Continent at the Game of Grab." To what a pass have we come when John Bull's grandchildren thus satirize his methods !

Another characteristic of the traditional John Bull was his serene contentment with things as they are. He was, as Sydney Smith said, " delighted with every existing institution and almost every existing circumstance." Such a one was Byron's typical John Bull :—

> He liked our taxes, when they're not too many ;
> He liked a sea-coal fire, when not too dear ;
> He liked a beef-steak, too, as well as any—
> Had no objection to a pot of beer.

Fifty years later Whyte-Melville, another social critic who saw life from the top, said of his typical Englishman : " He shaved scrupulously, drank port wine, and believed in the *Times*." To-day an Englishman may be as hairy as Esau ; his doctor assures him that port is poison ; and

D

he has views about the Northcliffe Press. He travels—or did before the War—and comes back with unnatural preferences for German stoves or Italian wood-fires ; thinks a skinny chicken and thin Moselle the true diet ; and is more than half inclined to prefer bureaucracy to self-government.

John Bull honestly despised all foreigners. Lord Palmerston was never more typically and representatively British than when he called Germany " that country of d——d professors." We were reared from our cradles in the creed that " Foreigners don't wash " ; and that statement seemed to hold the key of all international perplexities. We believed absolutely that no foreigner could ride, row, or shoot ; and, in spite of a good deal of experience to the contrary, we half believed that foreigners could not fight.

Even darker suspicions of his European neighbours haunted the unregenerate mind of John Bull. Foreigners were conspirators. Foreigners were debauchees. Foreigners were either idolators or atheists. I have heard that, after my great-uncle, Lord William Russell, was murdered by his Swiss valet, it was for many years impossible for a foreign servant to get a place in London.

A greatly increased acquaintance with the world outside England has modified these insular prejudices of the traditional John Bull. We have been forced to admit that foreigners can fight and Colonials ride. We have learnt to behave ourselves with comparative decency in foreign churches. We no longer denounce the Roman Catholic religion as "a lie and a heathenish superstition." America no longer has occasion to complain of that "condescension" on the part of English people which once stirred Lowell's indignation. It is chiefly in reference to Ireland that John Bull still vaunts himself with offensive superiority.

Long ago Matthew Arnold pointed out that one of the chief reasons for the eternal misunderstanding between Ireland and England was the fact that the English were represented in Ireland chiefly by people like Murdstone and Quinion in *David Copperfield,* and by the products of Salem House and Mr. Creakle. " The Irish people," he said, " are capable of feeling thoroughly the attraction of the power of manners," but they do not feel it in the case of those who compose the English garrison. " The genuine, unmitigated Murdstone is the common middle-class Englishman, who has come forth from Salem House, and Mr. Creakle. He is seen in full force, of course, in the Protestant north ; but throughout Ireland he is a prominent figure of the English garrison. Him the Irish see, see him only too much and too often ; and he represents to them the promise of English civilization."

Thirty years have passed, and, as far as his relations with Ireland are concerned, John Bull remains the same graceful figure that Matthew Arnold knew so well. All this time he has been governing Ireland, with the results which we saw at Easter 1916 ; but perhaps he is now approaching the end of his reign.

52

VI

M.P. OR DELEGATE?

"THE Union of Democratic Control" is
a body about which I am very imperfectly
informed. In so far as it seeks to bring
the war-making and treaty-making powers
of the Crown under the cognizance of
Parliament, I am at one with it ; for that
is a change in our constitutional arrangements which I have always favoured. There
may, however, be. points in the policy
of the Union to which I could by no
means subscribe ; and I cannot be surprised that my friend Mr. Charles Trevelyan should find himself at issue with
his constituents. If I were a voter in
the Elland Division I think it probable
that I might be obliged to give my
representative what is called "a bit of
my mind "—even that proverbially disagree-

able " bit " which conscientious people reserve
for their erring friends.

But I am bound to say that, in my
opinion, Mr. Trevelyan, in replying to his
Liberal Association, took exactly the right
line, and stated the constitutional relation
between Member and Constituents with force,
dignity, and good temper. The parallel,
tempting enough in some respects, which
the *Times* drew between Mr. Trevelyan's
letter and Mr. Gregsbury's reply to " his
old friend Pugstyles " fails in one all-
important particular. According to the
unchallenged statement of the deputation
which invited Mr. Gregsbury to resign his
seat, that legislator had broken all the
pledges on the strength of which he had
been elected. Mr. Trevelyan seems to
have broken none. He tells us that his
votes and speeches have been in exact
accordance with the declarations which he
made when he was elected, and I have
n seen his statement contradicted. It
may be true that his present actions are
distasteful his constituents ; but, unless

it can be shown that they are inconsistent with his pledges given at his election, the constituents have no right to demand his resignation.

Here, I take it, is the difference between a Member of Parliament, and the Delegate of some alliance or confederation. The delegate, I believe, undertakes to vote as the body which elects him may from time to time desire. He abjures private judgment, and makes himself a voting-machine. The Member of Parliament is bound only by the professions which he made when he sought election. He secured his majority by professing such and such convictions; and, so long as he maintains them and acts upon them, he is fulfilling his compact with the constituency. The constituents may change their minds, but they have no right to blame him because he stands fast to what he professed. Their opportunity comes with the next election. Then they can say, in the effective form of action : " The opinions which you hold are no longer ours, and we must seek a representative who agrees with us." Our political history abounds in such severances, and they imply no discredit to either side. For example, no one alleged that Gladstone, in the Parliament of 1859, violated the pledges on which he had been elected by the University of Oxford, or that, in the Parliament of 1865, he had broken faith with South Lancashire. There were a great many of his constituents who extremely disliked his votes in both Parliaments ; but no one asked him to resign. A disaffected constituent who had ventured on such a suggestion would have been promptly challenged to show the violated pledge ; and, failing to do so, he would have received a lecture on the relations between the representative and the represented which would have enlarged his constitutional knowledge.

In both cases, the constituency changed its mind during the life of the Parliament, and, when the day of reckoning came, dismissed its Member, though he was the foremost man in the Liberal Party. But no one ever suggested that Gladstone ought to resign before the Dissolution, because the opinions which were popular at his election had since lost their popularity. John Bright knew very well that his opposition to the Chinese War was unpopular in Manchester; but he never dreamed of resigning his seat. He had been elected as an advocate of peace, and he stood his ground till Manchester dismissed him. To take a more recent instance, the same difficulty beset the Liberals who in 1885 had been returned as opponents of Home Rule. After the General Election, Gladstone's conversion was announced, and the Caucus decreed that all Liberals were to follow their leader. Some weak-kneed brethren succumbed to pressure; but men of robuster material said: "We were elected to oppose Home Rule, and we shall vote according to our pledges. We shall neither turn our coats nor resign our seats"—and the Election of 1886 in most cases ratified their decision. Exactly similar was the case of the Unionist Free Traders, who, when Tariff Reform

57

was broached, found that the wire-pullers expected them to renounce Free Trade. The stronger men stuck to their beliefs and their seats, and left the constituencies to decide the issue at the General Election of 1906.

Obviously and entirely different is the case of the M.P. who, having been elected on a certain confession of faith, changes his mind during the life of the Parliament, and finds that he can no longer pursue the policy to which he pledged himself. In such circumstances an honest man does not wait for representations from his former supporters. He resigns his seat, and appeals from the Caucus to the constituency. Thus the late Sir William Marriott, having been returned as a Liberal for Brighton in 1880, changed his opinions in 1884, resigned his seat, and was triumphantly re-elected as a Conservative; and, in more recent years, the same course has been pursued by Home Rulers who have turned Unionist, and Unionists who have turned Home Rulers.

58

If, then, Mr. Trevelyan had changed the opinions which at the last Election commended him to the Elland Division, he would be bound by propriety and right feeling to resign and offer himself for re-election. But, if he stands now where he stood then, he should keep his seat and vote, not as others wish, but as he himself thinks right. Surely no one will be so foolish as to suggest that Sir John Simon ought, because he has retired from the Cabinet, to retire also from Walthamstow. Lord Kitchener, in supporting the Compulsion Bill, suggested with admirable gravity, that men who doubted about their duty in the matter of military service would be only too glad to have their doubts settled for them by authority ; and what that gallant soldier thought about military service the Caucus seem to think about political duty. But there will always be a " remnant " who prefer to shape their own course, and who own no authority except conscience.

VII

SCAPEGOATS

FROM time to time during the last two
years " scapegoats " have figured prominently
in the newspapers. One day Lord Derby
gave us his opinion of these long-suffering
animals, and his way of handling them
suggests that the origin and significance
of the Scapegoat has lapsed out of sight.
Commenting on certain miscarriages in our
military administration, his lordship said that,
if the English people must have scapegoats,
they had better make scapegoats of themselves. It might tend to clearness of thought
if he would turn to the Book of Leviticus,
and would investigate the origin of a phrase
which, like so many images and aphorisms,
found its way from the Bible into our
common speech. He will find it in the
Day of Atonement, as enjoined by Moses

60

on the Israelites, and in the ritual of
the Tabernacle. The ceremonies of the
day were singularly elaborate and detailed,
and at a certain point the High Priest
presented two young goats at the door of
the Tabernacle, and cast lots upon them.
On one lot was inscribed " For Jehovah,"
on the other " For Azazel "—a mysterious
appellation on which commentators have expended volumes of curious learning. The
goat dedicated to Jehovah was killed, and
its blood sprinkled on the sacred shrine.
This done, the High Priest laid his hands
on the head of the goat " for Azazel,"
and confessed over it all the sins of the
people. The goat was forthwith led into
the wilderness, into " a land not inhabited,"
and was then let loose.

There the prescribed observance ends.
The sin-laden goat vanishes into the unseen. It is true that the genius of
Holman Hunt depicted it, the most forlorn,
dejected, and broken-down creature in the
world, stumbling across an arid desert to
some unknown doom ; but that was only

a flight of fancy, and not less fanciful are the innumerable and contradictory interpretations which Jewish and Christian expositors have attached to the whole observance. Only one point seems to emerge quite clearly. An entire people cannot make scapegoats of themselves ; for it is of the essence of the symbolism that the selected victim bears vicariously the sins of others, and suffers for wrongdoing in which it has had no part.

There is something impressive and instructive in the fact that the popular imagination of four centuries has fastened on the Scapegoat, and has disregarded the goat that was sacrificed. Is it fanciful to read in this discrimination the tacit belief that disgrace and exile and contemptuous oblivion are heavier evils than the sharp stroke of death?

I have spoken of four centuries, for it is only since the translation of the Bible that "The Scapegoat "—*caper emissarius*, as the Vulgate calls him—has become familiar to English thought and speech. But the tendency, when things go wrong, to seize upon some inoffensive victim and hound him to destruction, is a good deal older than the Reformation, and will probably survive the twentieth century. " I have loved righteousness and hated iniquity ; therefore I die in exile," is a cry which, since Hildebrand uttered it, every age has re-echoed ; and the irritated populace has not always stopped short at exile and the image of the Scapegoat, but has preferred the shorter method of sword or axe or stake. Tyrannicide has had its apologists —Shakespeare, Milton, Byron, Shelley, and even the young Disraeli ; but tyrannicide implies a tyrant, and a tyrant justly suffers for his misdeeds. The Scapegoat is the man who suffers, not for wrongdoing of his own, but because others have done wrong, and the public temper is inflamed. Savonarola and Molinos were scapegoats in the truest sense of the phrase, each bearing the sins of a licentious and con-science-stricken age. Louis XVI expiated in his own unoffending person the accumulated crimes of a corrupt dynasty. The scapegoat of American slavery was Lincoln, who abolished it, and died a victim to the rage of the baffled slave-owners. The scapegoat of Russian autocracy was Alexander II, who liberated the serfs and was assassinated by the Nihilists. The scapegoat of English misrule in Ireland was Lord Frederick Cavendish, than whom Ireland never had a truer friend.

I have spoken, so far, of countries more or less remote from our own; but in the assertion of our own liberties we too have made free use of scapegoats. How far Charles I suffered for sins not his own is a question which Debating Societies will discuss to the end of time. James II, vanishing by night into exile and oblivion, and bearing with him the iniquities of all the Stuarts, was a scapegoat with a difference; for, though he suffered vicariously, he suffered for his own sins as well.

I turn from heroic and historic examples to the homely politics of the present day. Our wonderful Constitution has cleverly

64

adapted itself to changed conditions, has made all rough dealing with crowned heads unnecessary, and has provided an official scapegoat whenever the need for such a victim arises. On this point we can have no safer guide than Gladstone, who played the part of Scapegoat more than once—" In every free State, for every public act, some one must be responsible ; and the question is, who shall it be ? " Gladstone answers : " The Minister, and the Minister exclusively," and it is to be observed that when he says " The Minister," he means the Prime Minister, though, when he wrote, that title had not been, as it is now, officially recognized. He thus expounds the difference between the Prime Minister and his colleagues : " The head of the British Government is not a Grand Vizier. He has no powers, properly so called, over his colleagues ; on the rare occasions when a Cabinet determines its course by the votes of its members, his vote counts only as one of theirs. *But they are appointed and dismissed by the*

Sovereign on his advice." The resignation of the Prime Minister has the effect of dissolving the Cabinet. The resignation of any other Minister only creates a vacancy. Here we see our Constitutional scapegoat. If things go wrong in this department or in that, it is idle to attack Mr. Secretary Taper, or his friend Tadpole, President of the Circumlocution Office. If Taper and Tadpole are incompetent or injudicious or disaffected, it is the duty of the Prime Minister, who recommended them for office, to recommend their dismissal. Unless and until he does so he must bear the responsibility for their misconduct; and even if he delays to act after the case is proved, his action, taken too late, will not relieve him of the responsibility. When the moment comes for the nation to act by a General Election, he will find himself driven into the dreary wilderness to keep company with the *caper emissarius*.[1]

[1] Alas! he had not to wait for the General Election.

VIII

DISAFFECTION AND ITS REMEDY

IT was, I think, Robert Southey who said :
" I am no more ashamed of having been
a Republican than of having been young."
The same boast, or confession, might have
been made, thirty years after Southey's
time, by men who were growing up in
the 'seventies of the last century. Echoes
of the older republicanism still lingered
in the political air. Algernon Sidney was
still quoted on platforms. The French
Revolution was cited as the birth of the
new world. The downfall of the Monarchies
in 1848 was remembered by men who were
still active in politics. Edmond Beales,
haranguing the Reform League in Hyde
Park, protested that he was not a " subject," but a " citizen." Bradlaugh rushed
about the country " impeaching the House

67

of Brunswick." Dilke and Auberon Herbert divided the House of Commons against the Civil List. The collapse of the Second Empire seemed to threaten older thrones. Mr. John Morley, in *Compromise*, protested against outward signs of reverence for royalty. Queer old democrats like Nieass of Chelsea (whom the *Times*, to his disgust, called " Niceass "), used to sit when the Queen's health was drunk, and keep their heads covered when the National Anthem was played. Ardent youths longed for the fast-approaching day when " the last king should be strangled in the bowels of the last priest " ; and even sedate publicists like R. H. Hutton, of the *Spectator*, gravely pronounced that Republican institutions were " more self-respecting " than those under which we live.

But, as the 'seventies advanced towards the 'eighties, this anti-monarchical sentiment was seen to waver, and then to disappear. The nearly fatal illness of the Prince of Wales at the end of 1871 had disclosed an unsuspected depth of national

68

feeling for the Crown, and the events of each succeeding year made that feeling stronger. Queen Victoria, emerging from her ten years' seclusion, acquired a popularity enhanced by reverence, which deepened and increased until she became, as it were, a divinity in her lifetime; and there were two personal forces in the political world which tended in the same direction. Disraeli's bizarre genius had always perceived that a sympathy between "the Monarch and the Multitude" was the strongest safeguard of the Throne; all his energies were employed to make that sympathy real, and he knew exactly how to play on the foibles of both the parties involved. On the other hand, Gladstone was just reaching the height of his power; he had been acclaimed as leader of the democratic party, so far as England knows anything of democracy; and at the same time he was almost an idolator of the Throne. Of all our national institutions, it was the one which he was most prone to idealize. "His sense of chivalry," says

Lord Morley, "his sense of an august tradition continuously symbolized by an historic throne, moved him as the sight of the French Queen at Versailles had moved the majestic imagination of Burke a century before. From beginning to end he stood sentry over the interests, whether profound and enduring or trivial and fleeting, of the ancient monarchy of this kingdom." When the two great political parties of the country are dominated by men so devoted to the monarchical principle as Gladstone and Disraeli, the murmurs of disaffection are hushed; and when, furthermore, the Crown is identified in the popular view with private virtue and public service, the anti-monarchical spirit finds little to feed on. When Queen Victoria died, it was justly enumerated among the triumphs of her reign that she had lived through, and had lived down, Republicanism.

One of the most thoughtful books on the philosophy of politics which have appeared of late years was the great Duke of Argyll's treatise on *The Unseen Foun-*

dations of Society. That those foundations are liable to incalculable disturbances is a truth familiar to all whose studies carry them below the surface of things ; and close observers think that just now they can perceive some disquieting vibrations. " Republic," " Republican," " Republicanism," are words which had disappeared from common parlance ; but within the last few months they have been heard again, and heard in unlikely quarters. In one respect we seem to have improved upon the manners of the last generation, for when people discuss the monarchy they discuss it only as an institution, and eschew the evil precedent of 1871, when Queen Victoria herself was not free from insult and reproach. It is observed that the men and women who speak rudely of King George V are not serious-minded citizens, but the raffish denizens of a certain section of so-called Society—(Mr. Richard Whiteing has described it in *The Yellow Van*)—who feel their own moral practice rebuked by the daily life of an immaculate and duty-loving Court. The serious people avoid personalities, and deal only with institutions. Rightly or wrongly, they believe that monarchy makes for war. They remember the evil deeds of Kings and Emperors; they forget the machinations of political conspirators like Bismarck; the financial pressure which forced Great Britain to occupy Egypt and desolate South Africa; the blundering diplomacy which has repeatedly led us to, and sometimes over, the brink of avoidable war. Republics, they say, do not make war. If Germany or Austria had been ruled by a President instead of an Emperor, Europe might still be at peace. They point to the infinite complexity of Royal relationships, and hint, or more than hint, that the King of the Hellenes would not have been allowed to cozen and browbeat the Allies if he had no near kinsfolk on more important thrones.

Then, again, the people who use this kind of language have apparently only realized since the war began that the blood of

72

our reigning house is almost exclusively German—for tiny indeed, and much diluted, is the drop of Stuart blood which the framers of the Act of Settlement discovered in the House of Hanover. For my own part, I hold that no psychology could be more erroneous than that which assumes that because a man is one's cousin one must love him and wish him success. But the critics who just now are canvassing monarchical institutions appear to believe that even the faintest consanguinity is a stronger bond than patriotism and public faith.

I was brought up by people who remembered the older generation of the Royal Family, and they always declared that Queen Victoria's uncles and aunts had lost all trace of Germanism, and alike in their appearance, their character, and their speech, were as typically English as that loved and lamented lady who was the mother of our present Queen. The Royal Marriage Act, limiting the free choice of English princes and princesses by artificial restric-

73

tions, was one of the most indefensible statutes which Parliament ever passed. It put difficulties, often insuperable, in the way of such alliances as had linked the Plantagenets, the Tudors, and the Stuarts to the English people ; and it helped to impress a foreign stamp on two generations of the House of Hanover. There is to-day a well-beloved young prince, as English in character as in face, who is serving England on the soil of France.[1] Let Providence grant him an English wife, and the last murmur of disaffection will be drowned in the cheerful chorus of national rejoicing.

[1] Written in 1917.

IX

REPUBLICANISM

MY paper on " Disaffection," when it
was originally published, brought me a
good deal of correspondence. This is all
to the good, for such topics are much the
better for free discussion. A question
which in substance has been asked by
several correspondents is this : " In what
section of the populace do you meet the
language of Disaffection, which you describe? " I reply : In the raffish 'fringe
of smart society, in the lower middle class,
and among metropolitan artisans. As far
as I know, the rural population has never
been touched by Disaffection. Having,
from my earliest childhood, been familiar
with agricultural labourers, their lives, their
prejudices, and their desires, I deliberately
consider them the most sensible portion of

the Body Politic. They know exactly the grievances under which they suffer, they have a shrewd notion of the possible remedies, and they do not trouble themselves with idle speculation. A long hereditary tradition of keeping their own counsel makes them uncommunicative to strangers and busybodies ; habitual contact with the realities of nature and of life makes them wisely indifferent to bombast. Certainly it is not in the rural population that I should expect to find Disaffection, in the sense in which I used the word.

To the sections which I enumerated above I ought to add—though it is only a minute sub-section—the little band of those who believe that the Legitimate Sovereign of this realm is to be found in Bavaria, and, therefore, that the actual monarchy has no moral claim on our allegiance. But these, who used to call Queen Victoria " The Dowager Princess Albert of Saxe-Coburg," are too few to count. Dante-like, we will regard them and pass on. But one of my correspondents, though disclaiming any sym-

76

pathy with the White Rose, yet advanced the curious theory that, if the direct line of the Stuarts had continued to occupy the Throne—in other words, if the Revolution of 1688 had never occurred—the monarchy would be stronger than it is now in the affections of the people. Speculations on the might-have-beens of history are always interesting ; but to imagine that James Francis, or Charles Edward, or Henry Benedict, would have established an abiding hold on the affections of England, seems to me the very topsy-turvydom of conjecture.

Private correspondence and public criticism alike have ratified my account of Republicanism as it existed here in the later 'sixties and early 'seventies of the last century. Mr. Herbert Burrows made the interesting statement that Bradlaugh held King Edward's illness of December 1871 to have put the clock back for fifty years. (I quote by memory.) But his victory over typhoid was not the only service which King Edward rendered to the cause of monarchy. His unfailing tact,

his genial courtesy, his dignity of bearing
on all ceremonial occasions, his love of
befitting splendour, and his unaffected sympathy with the social ideas of the English
people—all these things were elements in
his popularity, and enabled him to confirm
and consolidate our national loyalty. " Vive
la République ! " cried a not unfriendly
voice as he drove through the streets of
Paris. " Mais c'est pour la France," was
his prompt and smiling reply. There was
a world of meaning in that *Mais*, and
both countries apprehended it. One of
my correspondents said with perfect truth :
" The sentimental value of the Crown in
regard to the Dominions and Colonies is
undoubted. Would it hold equally with a
Republic? Take India—would the Princes
there bear cheerful allegiance to a politician
elected to be President? I trow not."

Another force which contributed to the
decay of Republicanism was the increasing
power and audacity of Capital. Observant
citizens saw the far-reaching and secretive
operations of Capitalism directed to the

attainment of political power, and often attaining it. They realized that any form of Government, other than a strictly hereditary Monarchy, would give infinitely enlarged scope to the power of mere wealth, and would create a new world of log-rolling and axe-grinding, of chicanery and intrigue, with the object of putting Lord X. or Mr. Z. in the supreme place.

John Bright once said, with characteristic sense : " The question between Monarchy and Republicanism was settled by our fore-fathers a good many years ago, and I see no reason to unsettle it." But, for reasons which I indicated in a former chapter, there has of late been some return, in certain sections of the Body Politic, to the idea of Republicanism. This my correspondents admit ; and some, not content with re-gretting, suggest remedies for Disaffection. One is that the King should establish himself in the centre of his Army. Could there be a worse suggestion? We all were gratified when the Sovereign found it possible, once and again, to visit his troops, for we knew the happiness which his presence would bring to men who deserve all the happiness which they can get. We were thankful when he returned in safety; and we know that the place assigned by Providence to an English Sovereign is in the centre of his people.

Another suggestion, not much wiser, is that the King's personal part in the business of the State should be made more conspicuous, and his individual action dragged into the " fierce light " of publicity. Let the answer be given in Gladstone's words : " In the ordinary administration of the Government the Sovereign personally is, so to speak, behind the scenes ; performing, indeed, many personal acts, but, in each and all of them, covered by the advice of Ministers, who stand between the august Personage and the people. . . . Sole action for the Sovereign would mean undefended, unprotected action ; the armour of irresponsibility would not cover the whole body against sword or spear ; a head would project beyond the awning, and would invite a sunstroke."

My own remedy for the disaffection, less or greater, which may have been engendered by recent circumstances, has already been humbly submitted. The only dissentients from it whom I have discovered are those curiously innocent people who write to the papers suggesting an alliance with an Italian or a French princess, forgetting the fundamental fact that for the Sovereign or the Heir Apparent to marry a Roman Catholic forfeits his right to the crown and absolves the English people from their allegiance. Let a wiser word from one of my correspondents close this chapter :—

The old objection of the influence of the wife's relations on affairs of State could hardly apply nowadays. A little malice among some sections in society would be inevitable ; it would count for nothing against the feeling of the mass of the country.

X

ROYALTY

SOME recent remarks of mine about Royal alliances have prompted questions. "What is Royalty?" asks a perplexed reader. "Is there a Royal caste? If so, what are its limitations? How do people get into it? Can they fall out of it? And if so, how?" To answer these questions with precision is impossible; but to illustrate their complexity is easy. We will begin at home, and then pursue the subject to the Continent.

In England the sole fountain of honour is the Sovereign. All ranks, titles, and precedencies are his creations, and all questions of Royalty are governed by relationship to the Crown. Thus we speak habitually of "the Royal Family," but the phrase is elastic, and is used with varying extensions. The larger extension, according to Blackstone, includes all those, whether male or female, who could, by any possibility, inherit the Crown :—" Such before the Revolution, were all the descendants of William the Conqueror, who had branched into an amazing extent by inter-marriages with the ancient nobility. Such, since the Revolution and the Act of Settlement, are the Protestant issue of the Electress Sophia, now comparatively few in number, but which, in process of time, may possibly be as largely diffused." Thus spoke a true prevision ; for, even if we omit from the calculation the other issue of George III, the descendants, male and female, of his granddaughter Queen Victoria, would furnish the population of a village ; and each of these illustrious personages, unless he or she should become or should marry a Roman Catholic, is in the legal succession to the Throne of England. If Queen Victoria's sons had died without issue, we should now be subjects of the German Emperor.

Such, then, is the wider extension of
" the Royal Family "; the more confined
sense includes only those who are within
a certain degree of propinquity to the
reigning Sovereign, and to whom, on
account of that propinquity, the law pays
a peculiar regard. Kinsfolk of the Sovereign outside that degree fall into the
rank of ordinary subjects. An Act of
Henry VIII assigns places in Parliament
and at the Privy Council to the sons,
brothers, uncles, and nephews of the King ;
but, beyond those degrees, the kinsfolk of
the Sovereign are entitled to no place or
precedence except what they may have
acquired—say, by inheriting a peerage or
a title. The mere fact of their descent,
in a more remote degree, from the Sovereign, gives them, in law, no precedence,
though custom willingly concedes what law
does not confer—" The Princes of the
Blood Royal have, as to precedence, a
movable and not a fixed status ; constantly shifting with the greater or less
propinquity to the actual Sovereign ";

and this status, being ruled by Act of
Parliament, cannot be altered by the Royal
Prerogative. What, then, is the position
of a man who, being closely related to
the Sovereign, is not son, brother, uncle,
or nephew?

The question arose in an acute form
when Queen Victoria married Prince Albert.
It was proposed to settle it by Act of
Parliament, giving him precedence over all
the Royal Family except the future Prince
of Wales ; but the difficulties in this way
of adjustment were so many and so grave
that the project was dropped. The Queen's
prerogative could not give him precedence
in Parliament or in the Privy Council, but
it was sufficient to give him precedence
elsewhere, and the good sense and good
taste of Society accorded due honour to
the Prince who shared the life, though
he could not share the Throne, of the
Sovereign. Matters of mere title, however,
are within the discretion of the Crown. The
sons and daughters of the Sovereign, and
the children of the Sovereign's sons, are

" Royal Highnesses " by birth ; but, when we get a little farther away from the Throne, the title of Royal Highness is acquired only by favour of the Sovereign. William Henry, Duke of Gloucester, the " Silly Billy " of so many memoirs, though he was a nephew of George III, was not a " Royal Highness " till he was made such by the King on his marriage with the King's daughter. The well-remembered and much-beloved Princess Mary, Duchess of Teck, being born a niece of William IV, was made a " Royal Highness " by her cousin Queen Victoria ; [1] and the Queen conferred the same honour on Prince Christian of Schleswig-Holstein when he married Princess Helena, and on Prince Henry of Battenberg when he married Princess Beatrice.

But, except by the courtesy of foreign Governments, these honours do not " carry " beyond the limits of the British Empire, and some difficulties connected with the

[1] This statement has been disputed, *et adhuc sub judice lis est.*

precedence of Prince Albert when he visited foreign Courts induced the Queen to confer on him a more distinctive title. In 1857 Charles Greville, then Clerk of the Council, wrote in his diary :—

> The Queen has made Prince Albert 'Prince Consort' by a patent ordered in Council, but this act confers on him neither title, dignity, nor privilege. He was already as high in England as he can be, assuming the Crown Matrimonial to be out of the question : and it will give him no higher rank abroad, where our acts have no validity.

In the autumn of the same year Greville made this note :—" Prince Albert has been to Brussels for the marriage of the Princess Charlotte, where he seems to have made his first experiment of the effect to be obtained from his newly acquired title of ' Prince Consort of England,' as I see he signed the marriage - contract immediately after the Queen Marie Amelie, and before an Austrian Archduke."

According to English law, no man acquires rank from his wife. If one of what John Bright called " the numerous and respect-

able family of Smith," marries a peeress
in her own right, he remains Mr. Smith,
though his son will be a peer when the
mother dies. Thus, as we have said before,
marriage with Queen Victoria's daughters
did not make foreign Princes Royal until
the Queen conferred the rank, and the
Dukes of Argyll and Fife were no more
Royal after their marriages than before.
The most striking illustration of this rule
is given in the Queen's own words :—" It
is a strange omission in our Constitution
that, while the wife of a King has the
highest rank and dignity in the realm after
her husband assigned to her by law, the
husband of a Queen Regnant is entirely
ignored by the law."

A woman by marrying acquires her
husband's rank, and this principle has
been repeatedly asserted in English history. Henry IV married Mary de Bohun ;
Edward IV married Elizabeth Widville ;
Richard III married Anne Nevill ; and
each of these wives shared her husband's
rank. Henry VIII four times married his

subjects, and, though they were not happy wives, they were unquestioned queens. The ill-conditioned Prince who became James II married the Chancellor's daughter, and the observant Pepys noted the superlatively royal demeanour of the lady who had recently been Anne Hyde—" At White Hall we saw the Duchess of York sitting in state, while her mother stood beside her." Horace Walpole, describing the first visit paid to Strawberry Hill by his niece, Lady Waldegrave, after she had married the Duke of Gloucester, says : " I flew down to the front door to kiss the hand of my Royal niece " ; and instances nearer to our own time may be found in the case of Her Royal Highness the Duchess of Albany, who, before her marriage, was Her Serene Highness Princess Helen of Waldeck-Pyrmont, and, even more con- spicuously, in that of our gracious Queen, who before she married was Her Serene Highness Princess Victoria Mary of Teck.

So far I have spoken of Royalty as it is known to the law and custom of England ;

but, when we come to dealing with its foreign manifestations, the problem becomes more complicated. Here, at any rate, we have to deal with an historic, hereditary, and continuous line, and with usages handed down to us unbroken through the vicissitudes of a thousand years. But, when we turn to the Continent, we see the principle of Royalty agitated and perplexed by repeated revolutions. When Napoleon I conquered Europe, he redistributed its thrones : the descendant of one of his marshals is King of Sweden, and the House of Bernadotte has married into the Royal Family of England. The history, ancient and recent, of the Bourbons, whom Napoleon dethroned, we all know, and no one can dispute their royalty ; but to-day England records an equally respectful welcome to the descendants of Philippe Egalité, and to the august lady who, born Eugénie de Téba, shared from 1850 to 1870 the most splendid throne in Europe, and to-day watches, from her quiet retreat at Farnborough, the gallantry of France.

What, then, is the reply to the questions with which this chapter began? Royalty is, in its wider sense, the whole family, however remote, of one who is or has been a Sovereign; in its narrower sense, the close kinsfolk of a Sovereign now actually on the throne. There is no such thing as a Royal " caste," for in England, time out of mind, our Sovereigns and Princes have intermarried with families not Royal; and, abroad, revolutions and wars and congresses and treaties have admitted into " the Family of Princes " a variety of potentates whose ancestors two hundred years ago were occupying the lowliest of private stations. But for those who are born, or have made their way, into the " Family," is it possible to fall out of it? In the despotically - governed Empires of Austria and Russia a morganatic marriage was a way of exit; but English law knows nothing of morganatic marriages. Here a marriage is lawful or unlawful, and there is no middle term. Should H.R.H. Prince Cophetua wed a beggar-maid, with the

consent of the Crown, Princess Cophetua
is Royal and their children are heirs to
the Throne. Should he marry without it
(as the Duke of Sussex twice did), he
does not cease to be Royal, but his wife
does not become Royal, and their children
have no right of succession. When a revolution upsets a foreign country, and replaces
its monarchy by a republic, or its kingdom
by an empire, the deprived Princes are
Royal or Imperial still. It is difficult to
become Royal ; but, having once been Royal,
to become anything else is still more difficult.

P.S.—The foregoing observations are strikingly illustrated by the King's decision on foreign titles published
to-day— June 20, 1917.

XI

DICTATORSHIP

W. G. WARD—" Ideal Ward " of the Oxford Movement—was the most enthusiastic of ultramontanes. When a more moderate friend complained of the Pope's tendency to exalt pious opinions into Dogmas of Faith, he replied : " I should like dogmas to be like rolls—a fresh one at breakfast every morning." If, for dogmas regulating faith, we substitute decrees regulating conduct, we now have exactly the breakfast-table which Ward desiderated. We have a fresh decree every morning.

But people who bear my name have an hereditary objection to this state of things. When a panic-stricken Government interfered with the right of public meeting, and proposed to abolish *habeas corpus,* Lord John Russell said to the unreformed House of Commons : " We talk much—I

93

think a great deal too much—of the wisdom
of our ancestors. I wish we could imitate
the courage of our ancestors. They were
not ready to lay their liberties at the foot
of the Crown upon every vain or imaginary
alarm." A century later, another Government
(alarmed, I am bound to say, with better
reason) produced the Defence of the Realm
Bill, and, under the pressing exigence of
war, Parliament passed it into law without
noticing the extraordinary latitude of a clause
which placed all civil freedom under the
domination of executive authority.

While Lord John Russell protested against
unnecessary abridgments of liberty, he protested not less vigorously against the inter-
vention of Militarism in political affairs :—
" A Standing Army which destroyed the
freedom of England . . . would appear in
the shape of a Guardian of Order ; it would
support the authority of the two Houses
of Parliament ; it would be hostile to none
but mobs and public meetings, and shed
no blood except that of labourers and
journeymen." From such a " Guardian of

Order " all lovers of Freedom must pray to be delivered.

It should be the object of all reasonable people to be governed as little as possible. The gradual evolution of representative self-government has expressed the resolve of civilized men to manage their own affairs and live their own lives, with the least possible interference from above or from outside. To-day the chief opponent of this resolve is Bureaucracy, which had long been trying to undermine self-government, and to set up the ideal of being governed as much as possible, in opposition to the older and better ideal of being governed as little as possible. The war, in addition to other and more obvious mischiefs, gave Bureaucracy an immense increase of strength. Every week sees the creation of some fresh office, and of a staff employed in executing that office's behests. There are some forms of lower life in which, if you detach a part from the whole, the part detached has the power of living and propagating itself. Even so with

95

Bureaucracy. The Circumlocution Office is broken up into a dozen departments. An energetic official is placed at the head of each, and goes to work with a will, fulfilling Ward's ideal, and issuing decrees, like hot rolls, every morning.

In old days, when the Cabinet system was still in force, we knew that the Government as a whole was answerable for actions done in its name; and that a blunder or a crime committed by one department involved the 'fate of the whole Cabinet. To-day the oppressed subject knows not where to turn. If Mr. Podsnap or Mr. Perkup issues an absurd decree, or if the Minister for Turnip-tops urges a course which the President of the Board of Conscription disallows, to whom are we to appeal? If General Sir George Tufto, being "the competent military authority," forbids Family Prayers, on the ground that they may involve seditious proceedings or hinder the work of recruiting, can we invoke the Cabinet to defend our religious liberties? It is a dubious outlook, for the

DICTATORSHIP

Prime Minister is fully occupied in winning the war, and his Aaron and Hur have not made their fame by championing freedom. No one can admire Lord Milner's intellect more sincerely than I do; but his intense Germanism (I do not mean pro-Germanism) has made him, where freedom is concerned, "wrong with the intense wrongness which only an honest man can achieve, who has taken a false turn of thought in the outset, and is following it, regardless of consequences." Lord Curzon has been my friend for forty years; but to appeal to him on the ground that my civil or religious freedom was threatened by executive authority would, I fear, be about as hopeful an attempt as "to rear the jungles of Bengal on Salisbury Plain."

But, though the prospect is thus discouraging, I must admit that it might conceivably be worse. After all, the members of the Cabinet are civilians, and civilians, even though they have been Pro-Consuls, might yet understand, or

G   97

remember, what Civil Liberty means. Not so a military dictator. The military mind is constitutionally incapable of conceiving of Freedom, except as a pestilent mischief to be exterminated by whatever method comes most readily to hand. There is no need to ransack ancient or modern history for illustrations of my contention. At this moment, and for the last three years, the British nation has been struggling with all its might against the tyranny which German militarism is striving to enforce on the world. And yet there are some who say, in words or in effect : " Let us set a thief to catch a thief—a tyrant to fight tyranny— a dictator to resist dictatorship." Sooner than lose the war (and by losing the war I mean failing to crush Germany) I would consent even to this desperate expedient ; but in doing so I should feel an absolute conviction that, when the war was over—even when Berlin was turned into a dungheap—the Dictator would still be with us. Dictators, whether military or civil, have a wonderful power of sticking to their posts.

98

DICTATORSHIP

I began with a name which I at least venerate, and with the same name I end. When Louis Napoleon was President of the French Republic, he asked Lord John Russell to visit him at the Tuileries. He stuffed the honest English gentleman with all sorts of flummery about the national call which had summoned him to the Presidency; about the duty which he owed to France, and to his name; and about the irksomeness of the burden laid upon him. "That burden," he said, "is too heavy to be borne except for a very few years; and, when my term of office expires, you will see that I shall not offer myself for re-election." This, though true to the ear, proved false to the sense. In May 1852 he would have automatically ceased to be President. In December 1851 he committed an armed assault on the Constitution which he had sworn to uphold; killed some of his opponents and sent the rest to Cayenne; and established himself in a dictatorship which lasted, with some modifications of form, till he surrendered his sword at Sedan.

XII

THE WHIGS AND THE CONSTITUTION

Lord Palmerston once wrote a very impertinent letter to Queen Victoria. The Queen had desired his attendance at Windsor ; and he wrote from his house in Hampshire that he exceedingly regretted his failure to attend. He had got on his horse in Piccadilly, meaning to ride to Paddington Station, but by some mistake had gone to Waterloo instead, and had arrived at Broadlands instead of Windsor. There is a cheekiness about this way of excusing a breach of duty which justifies Disraeli's sneer at Palmerston's demeanour as that of " a favourite footman on easy terms with his mistress." But a Liberal reviewer, recalling the episode, made a doubly inept criticism when he described Palmerston's letter as " the most insolent document ever drafted by a member of the Whig aristocracy."

In the first place, Palmerston was not a Whig. Whether he could be rightly said to belong to an aristocracy is more disputable. I only know that the Whigs, with whom, when it suited his purpose, he allied himself, thought him very vulgar. But a Whig he was not. Gladstone, who did not much like Whiggery, though he often used Whigs, laid it down that "to be a Whig, a man must be born a Whig." But Palmerston was born and bred a Tory, and from 1807 to 1830 held office in Tory Administrations. The remaining thirty-five years of his life he spent, for the most part, in Whig Administrations, but he was not a Whig. The one thing in the world which he loved was power, and, as long as this was secured, he did not trouble himself much about the political complexion of his associates. " Palmerston does not care how much dirt he eats, so long as it is gilded dirt," was Gladstone's verdict ; and,

if " gilded dirt " be the right description
of office procured by flexible politics, Palmerston ate, in his long career, an extraordinary
amount of it.

This, then, was the reviewer's first blunder,
personal and particular. His second was
more general, but not less a blunder. The
" Whig aristocracy " did not " draft insolent
documents " for the perusal of the Sovereign.
The Whigs held (as Lord John Russell
told Queen Victoria) that all rulers are
liable to be removed for misconduct ; and
they had acted on that belief, directly
in 1688, indirectly in 1714. But, when
once they had displaced an offending
dynasty and installed another, they treated
the occupant of the throne with all traditional respect. Not even the mighty
Chatham, whose hooked nose could be seen
between his knees when he did obeisance
to George III, could have comported himself more reverently towards the Crown
than the Greys and Spencers and Russells
of the succeeding century. The very
fact that they had imported the House of

Hanover into this country made the Whigs doubly solicitous that the new dynasty should lack nothing of the " divinity " that had " hedged " its predecessors.

The Whigs were originally a group of great nobles, in whom the possession of rank and wealth had not extinguished the love of civil and religious freedom. They had little taste for ' revolution, but less for tyranny ; and, when the fatuous policy of James II convinced them that as long as he was on the throne there was no security for the old-established freedom of the realm, they had no scruple about inviting his daughter and son-in-law to take his place. At the same time they sedulously abstained from rash and unheeded innovation. They knew, as Machiavelli had known before them, that nothing so much tends to give stability to a change in government as scrupulous adherence to historic forms and venerable institutions. So, instead of indulging in raw abstractions and philosophies of statecraft, they contented themselves with confirming, by solemn statute, the ancient liberties of England, and protesting against the particular violations of those liberties which James II had committed. They proclaimed to the world that James, having broken the understood contract between King and people, having violated the fundamental laws of the realm, and having withdrawn himself out of the kingdom, had abdicated the throne ; and they invited William and Mary to fill it.

The fundamental principle of Whiggery was resistance to arbitrary power. The very phrase has now an archaic sound ; but, when it was originally coined, it expressed a very real and threatening danger ; and though, from the accession of the House of Hanover onwards, that danger was sensibly diminished, yet the Whigs never lost sight of the fact that circumstances might arise which would again make resistance a duty. Their favourite toast was : " The King, and may he never forget those principles which placed his family on the throne." They consistently held and taught the doctrine that there must be, in every free State, an

104

extreme remedy against the abuses of authority. When Edmund Burke, originally a Whig, had been thrown off his mental balance by his horror of regicide, he made this particular dogma of Whiggery the subject of one of his most vigorous protests :—" I confess I never liked this continual talk of resistance and revolution, or the practice of making the extreme medicine of the Constitution its daily bread. It is like taking periodical doses of *mercury sublimate*. It renders the habit of society dangerously valetudinary." Burke made his great appeal " from the new Whigs to the old." A Whig who was born in 1792 he would have considered a very new Whig indeed. Lord John Russell, who was born in that year, has never been reckoned among revolutionary politicians ; but he laid down in 1826, and reaffirmed forty years later, the doctrine of an " extreme medicine " for a possible disorder :—" If the King abuses a just, or attempts to exercise an oppressive, power, the representatives of the people have the right to refuse the money required to carry on the government." After enlarging on this theme, he continues :—

This power, it is quite clear, would enable the House of Commons, if so disposed, to declare themselves the sovereigns, and to take away every efficient prerogative from the Crown ; but such is the moderation of the English people that they have never desired so formidable an increase of their own power or that of their representatives. At the Revolution, when the whole question was open, they did not take away a single grain of the powers necessary to maintain the monarchy. So, at the present day, the true reason why the Crown maintains its prerogative unimpaired lies in the temper of the nation. The country has a deep-rooted affection for kingly government, and would highly resent any attempt to change or destroy this keystone of the Constitution.

There spoke the authentic voice of Whiggery, and I believe that it was also the voice of truth. In spite of what I wrote on page 71, there is no general desire in England for an alteration in the form of government ; but, when we look through forms into realities, there seems to be a good deal of ignorance about the actual working of the Constitution. To put it plainly, a great many people do not know how they are governed. They seem to believe that the Sovereign is a mere figure-head ; and are half-amazed, half-indignant, when they are assured that he or she—for I am not thinking of any particular Sovereign—exercises any influence on the affairs of the State. It is difficult to understand how this strange misconception of the functions and uses of the Crown have survived the publication of all the volumes of Royal and Ministerial correspondence which have appeared within the last fifty years. But so it is, and the explanation must be that we are neither a reading people nor an imaginative people. If we were imaginative, we should be better able to realize that some of the most important transactions in life go on out of sight ; and, if we read, we should know that Queen Victoria—to say nothing of her successors—exercised for sixty years a vigilant, direct, and powerful influence on domestic and foreign policy. In the transaction of public affairs, the Sovereign

has, as Gladstone pointed out, more than one advantage over his Ministers. He is permanent, while they are fugitive ; he speaks from a vantage-ground unapproachably higher ; he can take a calm and leisurely survey, while they are worried with the preparatory stages and the pressure of countless details. He must therefore be a weighty factor in all deliberations of State. Every discovery of a blot, which his studies in the domain of business enable him to make, strengthens his hands and enhances his authority. Now all this is obviously true, as far as it goes ; but, to make it a full presentment of the truth, we must recur to that prime creation of the Whigs—the doctrine of Ministerial responsibility. " There can," said Gladstone, " be in England no disloyalty more gross, as to its effects, than the superstition which affects to assign to the Sovereign a separate, and, as far as separate, transcendental, sphere of political action. . . . In the face of the country, the Sovereign and' the Ministers are an absolute unity." And
108

WHIGS AND THE CONSTITUTION
=================================

this unity can only be dissolved by one
of two occurrences. It may be dissolved
by the decision of the Sovereign to change
his Ministers ; or it may be dissolved
by the refusal of Ministers to bear responsibility for acts of which they dis-
approve. In either of these contingencies—
dismissal or resignation—the responsibility
for a great and critical act falls, for the
moment, on the Sovereign ; but only for
the moment. The incoming Minister takes
over, by his acceptance of office, the responsibility which the Sovereign has incurred.
When in 1834 William IV dismissed the
Government of Lord Melbourne, he acted
within his constitutional right, and his immunity was secured by the action of Sir
Robert Peel in accepting the vacant post.
When, in 1839, Melbourne resigned, and
Queen Victoria sent for Peel, she refused
to take a step—the dismissal of the Whig
ladies of her Court—which Peel considered
essential to the formation of a stable Government. But the Whig Ministers, though
they had resigned, were waiting in the

109

background, and, by resuming office, they again secured the immunity of the Sovereign.

I have, of set purpose, chosen two incidents removed by a long distance of time from modern controversies. I might illustrate the doctrine of Ministerial responsibility by abundant citations from the literature of Whiggery ; and I confirm it by yet another quotation from one who was not a Whig :—

> The Crown has large prerogatives, endless functions essential to the daily action, and even to the life, of the State. . . . They are entrusted to men who must be prepared to answer for the use they make of them. The ring of responsible Ministerial agency forms a fence round the person of the Sovereign, which has thus far proved impregnable to all assaults.[1]

---

[1] W. E. Gladstone, "Gleanings," vol. i.

XIII

FRANCE IN ENGLAND

ENGLAND and France are fighting side
by side against a common foe; and the
Republican Band of France has been received with public honours by the Lord
Mayor of London.[1] There is nothing very
sensational in this plain statement of the
fact; but its historical implications should
not be overlooked.

In October 1816 the French Revolution,
which in its successive phases held Europe
in awe for a quarter of a century, had
been laid to rest. Five years before,
the progress of Bonaparte had seemed
to Englishmen " as swift and as terrible
as the lightnings of God." But now
" the gloom of his glory " no longer " o'er-
shadowed the earth "; he was a beaten

[1] Written in October 1916.

III

man, caged at St. Helena. The Bourbons had returned, as it seemed permanently, to the throne of France. By common consent people agreed to regard the Revolution as merely a past event; and, freed at length from the terror which had so long obsessed them, they sate down to reason quietly about its causes. Some of the conclusions at which they arrived were quaint enough. Perhaps, after the lapse of a century, we are in a better position to trace the sequence of events which connects the downfall of the French Monarchy with the development of constitutional government at home.

The celebrated saying of Napoleon that, if Rousseau had never lived, there would have been no Revolution, contained, in spite of its exaggerated form, an unquestionable truth. What distinguishes the French upheaval from other political movements is that it was directed by men who, having adopted a speculative conception of political right, propagated it with all the

112

fanatical enthusiasm and proselytizing
fervour which one commonly associates
with a religious belief. The sacred oracle
of these revolutionists was the *Contrat
Social* of Rousseau, with its fundamental
distinction between Sovereignty and Government. Sovereignty, according to Rousseau,
resides inalienably in the whole mass of
the population, and no Government is legitimate which does not rest upon the election
of the whole people. So far, Rousseau's
teaching accorded with that of English
Whiggery, but he went a good way farther.
He taught that no act of even a properly
constituted Government is valid unless the
people have directly sanctioned it. Representatives are mere delegates, with no right
to act or vote except as they are instructed. The utmost that can be said
of any authority is that it is a provisional
form of administration, existing until the
people shall otherwise determine. Whenever the people are lawfully assembled in
a public body, they resume the functions
of sovereignty ; the jurisdiction of govern-

H   113

ment ceases, and all executive power becomes null and void.

These theories entered into the heart's blood of French thought and feeling. Rousseau's disciples learned that no authority could be legitimate which did not harmonize with their own transient desires ; that political power is not a trust, but a right ; that absolute equality is the first condition of good government ; and that Constitutions can safely be re-arranged on grounds of abstract theory, without reference to history, tradition, racial characteristics, or differentiating circumstances. The full significance of these theories was scarcely perceived until a group of men, more desperate than their teacher, translated them into practice. When that was done the effect was startling, was universal, and—what is more—was permanent. In 1816 Louis XVIII seemed to have restored his dynasty. In 1887 the Duc d'Aumale said to the present writer : " No member of my family will ever again sit on the throne of France. A

114

capable Bonaparte might have a chance ; but what I expect is a succession of Republics."

The intellectual unsettlement which heralded the French Revolution was promoted by the study of those systems of politics and philosophy which Voltaire had learned in England, and which, on his return to France, he naturalized among his countrymen. The impulse started from England, and to England it returned. The forces which revolutionized France re-acted on the internal system of the country from which they had been derived. The Revolution influenced English history, in the latter years of the eighteenth century, more powerfully than any other event ; it gave a completely new direction to the policy of Pitt ; it shattered and rendered ineffectual for a whole generation one of the two great parties in the State ; and it determined, for a like period, the char-acter and complexion of our foreign policy.

The capture of the Bastille was an act so startling and so dramatic that it in-

stantly arrested public attention, and the
events which immediately followed in rapid
and striking succession intensified and sus-
tained the excitement and the interest. All
over the country those events produced
their immediate and natural effect. Enemies
of religious establishments took courage
from the downfall of established religion
in France. Enemies of monarchy rejoiced
in the formal and public degradation of
a King and Queen. Those who had long
been labouring in the cause of Parliamentary reform saw, with glee, their principles carried to their utmost limits, and
expressed in the most uncompromising
terms, in the French Declaration of Rights,
and practically applied in the constitution
of the Sovereign Body in France.

Serious advocates of Republican institutions, mere lovers of change and excitement,
secret sympathizers with lawlessness and
violence, sedentary theorists, reckless adven-
turers, and local busybodies, associated themselves in the endeavour to popularize the
French Revolution in England and to

116

imbue the English mind with congenial sentiments. The flame of freedom spread far and wide, through high and low. The Dukes of Norfolk, Richmond, and Bedford, Lord Lansdowne and Lord Stanhope, held language about the Sovereignty of the People, such as filled the reverent and orderly mind of Burke with astonishment and misgiving. The Revolution Society, founded to commemorate the great doings of 1688, corresponded with the lovers of freedom in France, and proffered its alliance in a revolutionary compact which was to embrace all Europe.

Amidst all this hurly-burly, Pitt, who, whatever else may be said of him, was a very great ruler, maintained a steady and cautious reserve. Probably he foresaw his opportunity in the hopeless disruption of his opponents. That disruption was not long delayed, and when it came it rent in twain the party of Progress, and retarded the development of English liberty by at least twenty years. But the spirit which makes Revolutions is indestructible, though it waxes and wanes, embodies itself in various forms, and works by manifold methods. To-day Republican France is the sworn ally and the honoured guest of a land which has learnt to regard the Crown as the consecrated symbol of its political freedom.

II

IDEALS AND WAR

I

CONSCIENCE AND CASUISTRY

CONSCIENCE is, or should be, one of the commonplaces of existence. Yet whenever it makes a public appearance in the affairs of practical life, it is regarded as something new and strange—even offensive. Clumsy satirists make gibes about " the Nonconformist Conscience " or " the Conscientious Objector," and write of conscience as if it were necessarily a fraud, or at best a fad. To remedy this disordered thinking or feeling is the office of Casuistry. The word has an evil sound in the ears of the average Englishman, and that this is so is a matter for regret ; for the thing which, for want of a better name, we call Casuistry, is an absolutely necessary part of the equipment of every one who " makes his moral being his prime care."

121

POLITICS AND PERSONALITIES

My Roman Catholic friends must not be angry if I quote the opinion that "great discredit has been brought upon Casuistry by the overminuteness with which it has been pursued in the works of the Jesuits," and which has created in the popular mind the impression that Casuistry is merely a sophistication of the plain laws of right and wrong.

That Casuistry may be thus perverted I do not deny; but, in itself, it is simply the Science of Duty. Jeremy Bentham, who hated priestcraft and loved alarming words, called it Deontology; but he meant the same thing. The word is derived from the Latin *Casus*, and epitomizes what is conveyed by *Casus Conscientiæ*—Cases of Conscience. The Casuist is the person who studies, and attempts to decide, such cases. Every one who acts conscientiously must be a Casuist on his own account, and the degree in which he is so will depend partly on the circumstances of his life, partly on the keenness or dullness of his conscience, partly on his intellectual capacity to see things as they are and not as they seem to be. The laws of reason, the laws of society, the laws of revealed religion are the chief authorities, external to the intuition of Conscience, by which the course of duty in difficult cases must be settled. For although, in a simple life, duties are correspondingly simple, and the intuition of Conscience needs little help; yet there are few lives so free from complexity that puzzling questions of duty do not occasionally arise; and the more complex the life the more numerous must be its problems. Where duty is not self-evident, it can only be ascertained by a careful process of weighing one consideration against another. Take the most familiar of all illustrations: Is it a duty under all circumstances to speak the truth? Yes. But suppose a friend is sitting in your garden, and a lunatic armed with a carving-knife comes into the room and says: "I am sent by God to kill So-and-so— do you know where he is?" (and this is not an imaginary illustration). Is it a duty to reply: "Yes, I know he is in the garden"? Most people would say No; but whether they said No or Yes they would be practising Casuistry.

The principle which underlies the enquiry stretches far and wide. George Herbert says :—

> Every one hath not digested, when it is a sin to take something for money lent, and when not; when it is a fault to disclose another's faults, and when not; when the affections of the soul in desiring or procuring increase of means or honour be a sin of covetousness or ambition, and when not; when the appetites of the body in eating, drinking, sleeping, and the like be sins of gluttony, drunkenness, sloth, and when not; and so in many circumstances of actions.

The science of duty, or Casuistry, is simply the application of general laws to particular cases; and it is a science which every one, who is not content to live his moral life at haphazard, is bound practically, though perhaps informally, to study. It is perilous, as Bishop Westcott said, to "trust to an uncultivated notion of duty, for an improvised solution of unforeseen difficulties." The words, indeed, are modern,

124

but the same thought has always been present to grave minds, and has made a deep mark on English literature. Among our English writers on Casuistry were William Perkins—a name now wholly forgotten—and Joseph Hall, not widely remembered. To them succeeded John Donne and Robert Sanderson and George Herbert and Richard Hooker. Jeremy Taylor, gathering all that was best from his predecessors of every age and tongue, and adding to it the treasures of his own experience and imagination, enriched our literature with his *Ductor Dubitantium*, or *The Rule of Conscience in all her General Measures*. Two centuries later Frederick Denison Maurice became Professor of " Casuistry, Moral Theology, and Moral Philosophy " at Cambridge, and did all that genius and devotion could do to rescue the Science of Duty from the discredit into which it had sunk in an age of moral indifference.

Probably those people who read treatises, whether ancient or modern, on Casuistry,

are extremely few ; but no one who knows
anything about the inner lives and hidden
difficulties of his fellow-men can doubt
that the application of the general laws
of moral duty to particular cases is the
cause of perplexities, and to sensitive
natures of agonies, all the more torment-
ing because generally unacknowledged. We
need not go to books for illustrations of
my meaning. A politician finds himself
opposed to his party on a particular issue
—War, or Home Rule, or Disestablishment, or whatever else it may be. Is
it his duty to suppress his convictions on
the particular point, and support the party
with which on the whole he agrees? Or
ought he to ally himself with the party
which he believes to be, on the whole,
wrong, for the sake of one point on which
it is right? A young journalist, with his
daily bread to make, finds that the paper
for which he works has changed its attitude on some vital question. Should he
stifle his conscience and go on supporting what in his heart he believes to be the

wrong cause? A man who had once borne the King's Commission was forced to take a humble job in a stockbroker's office. The office was in a block of flats; a rival stockbroker had the flat below. The new clerk found that he was expected to pause on his frequent goings up and down, and to linger about the rival's door on the off-chance of catching a casual word from within which might be useful to his employer by disclosing the rival's operations. To resign meant ruin for mother, brothers, and sisters. What was the course of duty?

Alas! I am no *Ductor Dubitantium*, and I can only reply, in the most general terms, that the hard way is generally the right way. It was by gallantly 'breasting the Hill of Difficulty that Christian reached the chamber called Peace, whose window opened towards the Sunrising :—

This Hill, though high, I covet to ascend ;
The difficulty will not me offend ;
For I perceive the way to life lies here ;
Come, pluck up, Heart ; let's neither faint nor fear:
Better, tho' difficult, th' right way to go,
Than wrong, though easie, where the end is wo.

127

II

CONSCIENCE AND COURAGE

FOR a paper which will be read in Holy Week there can be no more appropriate subject than Conscience.[1] The highest exemplification of conscience which the world has ever seen was made at this season, and it sheds dignity on the humblest and even the most erroneous attempts to do what seems right without regard to consequences.

The Christian Church is founded on the action of conscience. To burn a pinch of incense in honour of the Olympian deities must have seemed a very small thing to the ordinary pagan, but conscience forbade the Roman Christians to do it; and so the blood of the martyrs became seed. Where the Christian populations writhe under the domination of Mohammedanism,

[1] Written in March 1917.

"many a tender maid, at the threshold of her young life, has gladly met her doom, when the words which accepted Islam would have made her in a moment a free and honoured member of a dominant community." She followed conscience, and paid the forfeit. Nearer home, men and women and boys and girls have died by fire sooner than accept a spiritual domination against which their conscience rebelled ; and, in times more recent and rather more humane, people whose reading of the New Testament was different from mine have faced imprisonment and the " spoiling of their goods " sooner than contribute to the support of a Church which in their judgment taught error. It would require, not an article but a very large book, to narrate the history of conscience and the courage which it inspires, and, if that book were faithfully written, there could be no nobler reading.

But every one must have observed that the mere mention of the word " conscience " —still more, the resolve to act on it when

I   129

it runs counter to popular prejudice—always
excites an insolent fury in those whose
sole guide is convention. When the Nonconformists declined to follow the leadership of a politician who had conspicuously
offended against the moral law, men of
the world, as they are called, poured
angry scorn on " the Nonconformist Conscience." When Dr. Clifford and his
followers announced themselves as " Passive
Resisters " to the Education Act, the scruple
of conscience which dictated their resistance
was made the subject of imbecile jesting.
And now, when a man declares that he
is a " Conscientious Objector " to military
service, the epithet, though it may be absolutely just, is invariably treated as a
synonym for hypocrisy and humbug. For
my own part, I have always held (and
said as long ago as 1883) that " there
are some causes, such as life and home
and freedom, for which the gentlest and
most humane of men must be prepared
to draw the sword ".; and to this belief
I hold unfalteringly. But I know by

experience that men fully as well entitled
to credence as myself affirm that their
conscience teaches them otherwise; and
to coerce them into doing what their conscience forbids, or to punish them for
not doing it, seems to be an act which
befits a Cæsar or a Sultan rather than
a Christian Government. I must confess
that, though I think the "Conscientious
Objector" entirely wrong, I have nothing
but respect for the courage with which he
submits to the physical and moral consequences of his action. However grave may
be his error, such a man has conspicuously
vindicated himself against the charge of
cowardice.

But that numerous crowd whose one
notion of government is bullying are apt
to reply: "How are we to know that the
man is really obeying conscience? Perhaps all the time he is only trying to
save his skin." Certainly, it would need
omniscience to be absolutely certain in
this, as in any other case. But, when
Parliament was stripping us of our liber-

ties, I thought that it promised an elaborate system of judicial enquiries, by which the honest scruples of conscience were to be distinguished from cowardly evasions of public duty. I confess that if I knew a man who had, in old time, held such hideous language as—" What we want is a jolly good war," and if I now saw 'him sueing for exemption on the ground that he objected to killing his fellow-men, I should without hesitation overrule his plea of conscience. But, where a man can show me that, before 1914, he had held that all war is unlawful, I should say : " You have proved your case. It is not for us who think otherwise to coerce you. Go in peace."

To illustrate my meaning, let me turn from the grave concerns of adult citizenship to a wise word of counsel which was urged long ago on boys. " As to fighting," said Tom Hughes, " keep out of it if you can, by all means. When the time comes, if it ever should, that you have to say ' Yes ' or ' No ' to a challenge to fight, say

'No' if you can—only take care you make it clear why you say 'No.' It's a proof of the highest courage if done from true Christian motives. It's quite right and justifiable if done from a simple aversion to physical pain and danger. But don't say 'No' because you fear a licking, and say or think it's because you fear God, for that's neither Christian nor honest." Which things are an allegory; and it carries a clear lesson for those who feel disposed to decline their share in that burden of military service which the country has laid upon them.

Cardinal Newman once magnificently said that Conscience is a King in its imperiousness, a Prophet in its predictions, a Priest in its benedictions and anathemas. If we are wise, we shall submit to that imperiousness, give heed to those predictions, desire those benedictions, and dread those anathemas. But while we thus profess to be disciples of conscience, we must be careful to remember that the discipleship of others may be fully as genuine as our own,

133

though it wear a different garb and speak with an unfamiliar accent. Our duty is to act, according to the best light we can get ; but we must remember that even the lights to us which seem clearest, are only " broken lights," and that the glib condemnation of others who see differently is as unwise as it is unjust. " Never," said Gladstone, " never let it be forgotten that there is scarcely a single moral action of a single man, of which other men can have such a knowledge, in its ultimate grounds, its surrounding incidents, and the real determining causes of its merits, as to warrant their pronouncing a conclusive judgment on it." Those are weighty words, appropriate to all times when passion is aroused, and to this time in particular.

Just after I had written the foregoing paragraph, I found (in Lady Newton's delightful book, *The House of Lyme*) these admirable words of John Bradshawe, the Regicide :—

As for the Quakers . . . I have but one rule for them, and for all that come before mee as Judge.

And that is the equall iust and impartiall Law of the Land, which directs and commands like Justice in like cases to all sortes of persons, And therein Quakers have their share as well as others.

III

THE TRUSTEES OF POSTERITY [1]

MY text is taken from the writings of a
political genius, whose opinions I did not
share, but whose gifts I profoundly admire.
Lord Beaconsfield says, in his fascinating
tale of *Sybil* :—

> We live in an age when to be young and to be
> indifferent can be no longer synonymous. We must
> prepare for the coming hour. The claims of the
> Future are represented by suffering millions, and the
> Youth of a Nation are the Trustees of Posterity.

If these words were true in 1845, they
are doubly and trebly true to-day. " The
Trustees of Posterity "—mark the phrase.
I propose to enquire what characteristics
should distinguish the young citizen who
takes his citizenship and its possibilities

[1] A Presidential Address to the " Young Britons "
Society.

seriously, and aims at becoming, as Lord Beaconsfield said, a Trustee of Posterity.

For my own part, I have not the slightest doubt about the characteristic which I should place in the forefront. The young citizen must be, first and foremost, a lover of Freedom—Heaven's best gift to the individual and to society. The liberty, which Milton loved, " to know, to utter, and to argue freely " — the liberty to act in things secular and sacred, in public and in private, according to one's own conviction of what is right—is the one incomparable good of life, the one priceless possession for which no earthly equivalent can be found, no conceivable boon be taken in exchange. And of this liberty the young citizen must accept only one limitation, and that is that the exercise of his own freedom shall not infringe the freedom of another. In that single, simple condition he recognizes the law which regulates, while it sanctions, the awful though glorious prerogative of Free Will. That one restriction the young citizen must admit as belonging to the very nature of liberty and to the elementary necessities of human society. He admits this one, but he will admit no more. Loving liberty himself, he desires to see it " in widest commonalty spread " among all his fellow-men, irrespective of race, colour, or creed.

Second only to Love of Freedom, we place in this ideal portraiture Faith in Progress. To believe that the world is going from bad to worse ; that each age and each year loses some old good and brings some fresh evil ; that every change in life, in thought, in society, is a deterioration ; that novelty is synonymous with mischief ; and that all apparent progress is essential retrogression—this may be a suitable creed for the aged and the timid, for jaundiced visions, and faded hopes, and failing health, and waning intellect ; but surely it is no gospel for young and vigorous and aspiring minds, for resolute wills and hopeful hearts, and natures which believe in and long to prove their own high capacities.

To believe that " the great mundane move-

138

ment," as Matthew Arnold called it, is on the whole towards good; that Christianity is not a colossal failure; that civilization is not a heartless sham; that, under the influence of both, the world is gradually but surely passing on towards a better age, and that we, in our several degrees and stations, can do something to accelerate its progress—this is a sentiment which ennobles human existence. This answers the question: " Is life worth living? " This, more than any other principle, except, perhaps, the kindred passion for freedom, has characterized in every age the gallant and generous souls who have led the great onward march of redeemed humanity.

We have spoken of Freedom and of Progress. There is something which is indispensable to both. A Trustee of Posterity must be a disciple of Order. He knows that, without order, the liberty of the stronger will inevitably and fatally override the liberty of the weaker, and thereby set at naught his primary canon—that one man's freed m must not infringe the freedom

139

of his brother-man. He knows that, without order, the progress in which he longs to assist will be, not a rhythmical march, but a riotous hustle, in which the weakest must go to the wall. Order is a condition precedent both to liberty and to progress.

Closely allied to the Love of Order is the Spirit of Reverence. To a generous nature, reverence is as natural as the passion for freedom or the impulse of progress. Our young citizen must be always on his guard against that miserable vanity, which attempts to magnify itself by depreciating all that has hitherto claimed the homage and the admiration of mankind. He knows that there is much, even for the youngest and cleverest of us, to learn from what " larger minds have thought out in calmer ages "—from " the long result of time "— from the general tendency and drift of human thought and experience. He reveres all human excellence. He recognizes the sign-manual of Heaven in human intellect. He sees the lineaments of a diviner

140

nature than his own in human goodness.
Industry, and energy, and courage, and
patience, independence of character, freedom of judgment, gentleness, self-control,
self-sacrifice—the dogged labour which gives
a lifetime to an obscure but beneficent
work ; the flash of genius which, in a
sudden moment, lights the path to fame—
these are the qualities, these the attributes,
which attract the homage of the young
citizen. But, with his whole heart, he spurns
and scorns the false gods of this world
which cry aloud for his worship. He has
no homage for wealth, except as a proof
of industry ; nor for rank, except as the
guinea-stamp of superior merit. He has
no reverence for man-made dogmas, foisted
by pious fraud on ignorance and credulity.
He has no respect for pretentious self-
assertion. He will not bow the knee to
any reputation, however high its pedestal
in the world's temple, unless he is persuaded that it has a moral title to stand
where it is. He claims the right to judge,
by his own conscience and reason, every

demand which is made upon his reverence.
But, when once that judgment is satisfied,
he has reverence in abundant store for
the object which is found worthy to receive
it. He knows that hero-worship is the
most graceful privilege of youth, and
he enjoys it unsparingly. He "lives by
admiration," as well as "by hope and
love."

Love of freedom, contempt for false pretensions, worship of intellect—these combine
to produce belief in Equality. The human
soul, made in the image of God, is the
one real object of reasonable reverence.
This reverence the young citizen pays. He
hates all artificial barriers between class
and class, the spirit of caste, the deifi-
cation of selfishness. He loves his brothers
and sisters in the human family. He
aims at Social Service. And the ideal of
social service is, first, to lighten the load of
existence for those thronging millions whose
one experience of life is a protracted
suffering; and then, as Wordsworth says,
"to add sunshine to daylight by making

the happy happier." However humble his station, however circumscribed his opportunities, the young citizen can always find some sort of social service ready to his hand. The poor, the weak, the hungry, the untaught, the overworked—all these send up their bitter cry, " How long? " and, in ministering to them, the young citizen knows that he is making his definite, though perhaps unnoticed, contribution to the social redemption of humanity. Truly said George Eliot—" The growing good of the world is partly dependent on unhistoric acts ; and that things are not so ill with you and me as they might have been is half owing to the number who lived faithfully a hidden life, and rest in unvisited tombs."

And here let me remark in passing that there is one clear, easy, and obvious department of social service. Sanitary reform is the first step towards securing happiness and health and length of days for those who, by their daily labour of hand or head, principally maintain the pre-eminence

143

of the race. The young citizen—the Trustee
of Posterity—is impatient of a state of
society in which healthy dwellings, and
unadulterated food, and pure water, and
fresh air, are the monopolies of the rich ;
and he can never rest till he sees, in
the neglected village or the squalid back-
settlements of the town in which he lives,
his own efforts contributing, however feebly,
to this form of special service. He must
do his part towards abolishing filth and eradi-
cating disease, and giving free scope to those
beneficent laws of Nature, which, " though
they were not revealed amid the thunders
of Sinai, are not less the commandments
of God."

This conviction of the sacredness of human
life—this belief that to maintain his own
life and the lives of others in health and
vigour is a paramount duty—naturally
leads our young citizen to a very definite
conclusion on the great subject of Peace
and War. He knows that we do not
necessarily sin against the sacredness of
human life when we strike down a foe in

144

battle, any more than when we consign a criminal to execution. He knows that there are causes, such as life, and home, and freedom, for which the gentlest and the most humane of men must be prepared to draw the sword.[1] But he is scrupulously anxious that the sword should never be lightly drawn. He will question with himself, once and again, whether any war which he is asked to sanction or support is really a just and necessary undertaking. He believes that the ruler of men, be he sovereign or statesman, who kindles war for selfish or dynastic ends, or for any miserable enterprise of annexation or self-aggrandizement, incurs an amount of guilt too terrible to contemplate. Not for an instant is he dazzled by the glitter of arms, or seduced from his calmer judgment by " the pomp and circumstance of glorious war." He remembers the words of the great American General to the

[1] This Address was delivered long before the present war began, and I reprint it for that reason.— G. W. E. R.

military students : " Boys, you think war
is all glory ; I tell you it is all hell.
He knows that it is a hell which brave
and good men must sometimes be prepared
to face ; but it must be faced earnestly,
resolutely, reverently, as men face death
and eternity. What he feels for himself
he feels for his country. He has no
ambition that England should figure as
the Swashbuckler of Europe. Rather it
is his glory to see her lead the way
in the enterprises of peace, in the sciences
which prolong life and the arts which
beautify it, and in the educative work
of rational self-government.

I have spoken so far of the young citizen's duty to others. But he has a duty
to himself, and this naturally falls into
three divisions, corresponding to the tri-
partite constitution of human nature—body,
mind, and soul.

1. The young citizen recognizes his duty
to his body. He will strive to keep it,
as nearly as may be, in a state of physical perfection. To this the reasonable use

146

of athletics will greatly contribute ; and remember that athletic training means also moral discipline. On this point listen to a word of guidance from St. Paul, who, like all effective teachers, illustrated his lessons by reference to the lives and habits of his hearers. Writing to his friends at Corinth, where the athletic games of the ancient world were brought to their highest perfection, he thus urges temperance and self-control (I quote from the Revised Version) :—" Know ye not that they which run in a race run all, but one receiveth the prize? Even so run that ye may attain. And every one that striveth in the games is temperate in all things. Now they do it to receive a corruptible crown ; but we an incorruptible. I therefore so run, as not uncertainly : so fight I, as not beating the air ; but I buffet my body, and bring it into bondage, lest by any means, after I have preached to others, I myself should be rejected."

Fashioning himself on this precept of a man who, whatever else he was or did, has made a permanent mark on the higher life of the world, the young citizen will do his best, by vigorous self-discipline, to make his body not a master, but a servant—the pliant instrument of a high purpose, a fit habitation for the moral and intellectual being that dwells within.

2. The young citizen has a duty to his mind. He reveres his intellect as a sacred trust. He nourishes it with the best that has been said and written. He corrects its imperfections. He strengthens its weak points. He seeks to fire and animate it by contact with minds greater than itself. He recognizes the fact that education is no mere matter of schooling or book-work; but a process which begins with the dawn of understanding and is never complete on this side of the grave, inasmuch as human life is inexplicable unless it is itself one long education for a better and fuller being. With an intellect thus sedulously tended and disciplined, with a range of knowledge thus constantly widening, with powers thus daily expanding to

148

a richer and larger life, the young citizen goes boldly forward amid shoals and rocks and contrary winds, knowing that, in intellect and conscience, he holds the golden charts which never yet failed the diligent and courageous mariner.

3. And the young citizen has a duty to his soul.

This discourse would be glaringly incomplete if I omitted to say a word about Citizenship and Religion.

Whatever be the form of religious profession to which the young citizen—the Trustee of Posterity—attaches himself; however keenly he may feel the " blank misgivings of a creature, moving about in worlds not realized "; this, at any rate, he will never do—he will never scoff at the idea of Religion. He will not ignorantly contemn that which has been, in every age, the guide in life and the strength in death of thousands of the world's best heroes. He will never dogmatize where Revelation is silent and Reason can only walk by tentative guesswork; nor strive

149

to enforce on others the creed which he has himself accepted. He will ponder deeply the significance of those two splendid texts :—" Ye shall know the truth, and the truth shall make you free " : " Where the Spirit of the Lord is, there is liberty." He will seek, with all diligence, a light for his own path, and conviction for his own intellect ; but he will gladly concede to his fellow-men the same unrestricted right of reasonable self-guidance which he claims for himself, and will walk, not only in humility and purity, but in charity with all the world. And if, as he recalls the great triumphs for mercy and civilization which Christianity in its heroic days has won, he sometimes feels a not unreasonable impatience at the present spectacle of Churches untrue to their faith, and lives which have fallen so far below their type, and feeble efforts for human good and indifference to human wretchedness ; then he will bethink him that, after all, the fault may be in the generation and the men rather than in the faith and the

150

system; and he will cry with Charles Kingsley—a man whose whole nature was stirred by the social and religious questionings of his own time :—

Wake again, Teutonic father-ages,
  Speak again, beloved primæval creeds;
Flash ancestral spirit from your pages,
  Wake the drowsy age to worthy deeds.

Tell us how of old our saintly mothers
  Schooled themselves by vigil, fast, and prayer;
Learned to love, as Jesus loved before them,
  While they bore the cross which poor men bear.

Tell us how our stout crusading fathers
  Fought and died for God and not for gold;
Let their love, their faith, their boyish daring,
  Distance-mellowed, gild the days of old.

The subject expands before us, and we must hasten to a close. It will not be supposed that I intend the sketch which I have placed before you for a finished portrait. I offer it rather as a rough, though I hope not inaccurate outline, which you must fill in and colour for yourselves.

And now you will ask, To what does all this tend? The character has been sufficiently indicated—in what is it to issue? Our young citizen has good gifts and great opportunities ; what is he to do with them?

Let me answer, in the first place, by negatives. There are some things which he most certainly will not do. He will not sacrifice his life and powers and aspirations to the Moloch of money-making. He will never regard poverty as a disgrace, or riches as a distinction. He will embark on no enterprise—political, commercial, professional—which he cannot reconcile with his notions of duty and honour. He will consider no occupation common or unclean or beneath his dignity, unless it implies dishonourable or immoral conditions. He will never content himself with a career of aimless idleness, " sitting down at life's banquet, and getting up without paying the reckoning." If circumstances give him immunity from daily toil, he will recognize in that immunity a special call to some voluntary work for his fellow-men, and

152

will sacrifice leisure and means to its fulfilment. If, on the other hand, circumstances bind him to active pursuits, he
will carefully choose the work for which
his peculiar powers seem best to fit him,
and in which his moral nature will have
fairest play. The work once chosen will
be steadily pursued and honestly wrought
with all his energies, but will never be
permitted to engross his heart, or deaden
his sympathies, or degenerate into an
organized selfishness. Whatever be his
handicraft, or trade, or profession, the
young citizen will remember that he is
something else, and something more important than craftsman, or tradesman, or
professional man. He will recollect that
he is a member of the human family,
and that every child of Adam's kin has
a claim on his sympathy and goodwill.
But a vague cosmopolitanism will not satisfy
him. He will bear in mind, every hour
of his life, at play, as well as at work,
in society as well as in church, that he
is a citizen of a great nation, and that

the enduring greatness of that nation must
be built, not on the abundance of its
material resources, but on the honour and
purity and courage of its sons. His is
that truest and holiest patriotism which
strives to express the love of country, not
by bluster or swagger or military vain-
glory, but by the sedulous cultivation in
ourselves and in others of the " righteousness " which " exalteth a nation."

"Here and here did England help me ; how can I
    help England ?"—Say,
Whoso turns as I, this evening, turn to God, to
    praise and pray.

The question was asked by a poet who
is one of our national glories, and a not
less glorious genius gave the answer in
prose. Said John Ruskin to the Undergraduates of Oxford :—

There is a destiny now possible to us, the highest
ever set before a nation to be accepted or refused.
We are still undegenerate in race—a race mingled
of the best northern blood. We are not yet dissolute
in temper, but still have the firmness to govern and
the grace to obey. We have been taught a religion
154

of pure mercy, which we must either now finally
betray or learn to defend by fulfilling. And we are
rich in an inheritance of honour, bequeathed to us
through a thousand years of noble history, which it
should be our daily thirst to increase with splendid
avarice, so that Englishmen, if it be a sin to covet
honour, should be the most offending souls alive.
. . . It is for you, youths of England, to make your
country for all the world a source of light, a centre
of peace ; mistress of learning and of the arts ;
faithful guardian of great memories in the midst of
irreverent and ephemeral visions ; faithful servant of
time-tried principles, under temptation from fond
experiments and licentious desires ; and, amidst the
cruel and clamorous jealousies of the nations, wor-
shipped in her strange valour of Goodwill towards
Men.

And now you will understand why I
have called my discourse " The Trustees
of Posterity " ; for, if I have not utterly
failed in the task which I proposed to
myself, I have shown that you, young
citizens of the present hour, are, in a
very real sense, Trustees for the greatness
and happiness and Christian honour of
England in the years that are to come—

And meanwhile, if these hours are dark, as indeed
in many ways they are, at least do not let us sit

deedless, like fools, and fine gentlemen, thinking the common toil not good enough for us, and beaten by the muddle ; but rather let us work like good fellows, trying by some dim candlelight to set our workshop ready against to-morrow's daylight.[1]

---

[1] William Morris.

IV

THRIFT

THRIFT is a text which has a mysterious
fascination for preachers. When I speak
of preachers I by no means confine myself
to men in Holy Orders, but include in
my purview all those who feel it their
duty to admonish their fellow-men, and
especially to exhort the poor. It is worthy
of note that in each succeeding age the
most strenuous preachers of thrift are those
whom Providence has placed beyond the
reach of poverty. When the Irish famine
broke out, the head of the English peerage
recommended the poor to rely on curry-
powder as a nutritious and satisfying food;
while the Council of the Royal Agricultural
Society, numbering some of the largest land-
owners of England, lectured the labourers
on the sustaining properties of thrice-boiled

157

bones. Archbishops and Bishops always try, like " Bishop " in *Little Dorrit,* to look as if they were rather poor than otherwise, and, when reformers like the Rev. Hubert Handley refer to the statistics in *Whitaker,* assure us that they have much ado to live in decency, and so can preach Thrift with a 'good conscience. Judges, too, strong in the secure enjoyment of £5,000 a year, are heavily down on extravagance ; and Ministers of State, while they exclaim with patriotic fortitude, " I draw my salary," tell us less fortunate citizens to save our half-sheets of paper and to discard butter in favour of margarine. It must be admitted that these consentient voices form a solemn harmony. " Be thrifty " ; " Economize " ; " Abandon your luxuries " ; " Live on half your income "—who can fail to be impressed by such commands as these, proceeding from monitors who pay super-tax? It behoves each one of us to look into his own expenditure, and see how far he can comply with these insistent hortations.

158

THRIFT

Swift is certainly not a writer to whom one would normally go for lessons of right living; but now and then he dropped a maxim which was worth remembering— " The stoical scheme of supplying our wants by lopping off our desires, is like cutting off our feet, when we want shoes." Indeed, the case might be put more strongly. One could, on an emergency, cut off one's feet, but no one can " lop off desires." We can, indeed, restrain desires, and refuse to gratify them. Every one who is not a criminal lunatic does so habitually. But desires can only be " lopped off " by some power which we do not control—a change in ourselves or in outward circumstances. The most that the strongest man can say about a conscious desire is : " It shall not master me." So, when the preachers of thrift declaim, they must not imagine that a hunting man can " lop off " his desire for a string of horses, or a working-man for a glass of beer, or a rich woman for a diamond necklace, or a shop-girl for a new hat. All that he or she can manage is : " I should like it, but I will go without it."

When once, from whatever motive, we face the salutary self-discipline of " going without it," the difficulty always is to know where one should begin. When the Tories cut down the £50,000 a year which the Whigs had proposed for Prince Albert, and fobbed him off with a beggarly £30,000, the Prince's comforters said that he must reduce his subscriptions. But this admirable method of making two ends meet cannot be universally followed, for it is not every one that has any subscriptions to reduce. Mr. John Dashwood, as we all know, had fully meant to give each of his three orphan sisters a thousand pounds ; but, after a careful survey of his financial position and a protracted consultation with his wife, he came to the conclusion that some help in moving their furniture, and a present of game at Christmas, would amply fulfil the requirements of the situation. When the bankrupt Duke of Buckingham was told that his means no longer permitted him to keep an Italian confectioner, as well as a French *chef* and an English roasting-cook, he exclaimed, in natural horror : " Good Gad ! Mayn't a man have a biscuit with his glass of sherry ? " It is really very difficult to draw the line between necessaries and luxuries. Even Professor and Mrs. Fawcett, under whom I sate in my youth, failed to draw it very clearly ; nor did we gain much assistance from the case (cited by them as a triumph of Political Economy) of the French workman, who " had at the same time the enjoyment of a pair of shoes and of a window." For those whose notions of decent living extend any further than this curious combination of comforts, the present moment is full of perplexity. We know that, as a nation, we are spending money at a rate which baffles comprehension ; and we also know that we shall inevitably have to pay our share of it. The only questions are : How ? and How much ?

Auberon Herbert, who was the most quixotic of politicians, was enthusiastically

in favour of voluntary taxation. He was
persuaded that, if only the Chancellor of
the Exchequer would plainly state the
national needs, every one would rush to
supply the money. The Chancellor would
get more—and much more—by free gifts
than by compulsion. Myself a worshipper
of Freedom, I feel that in the case supposed we might be trying the principle
a little too high. Not that I doubt my
fellow-citizens' patriotism; nor my own;
but my mind misgives me that one would
say, when Christmas came round: " Things
are rather tight with me this year. I
think we will let this demand stand over
for twelve months, and see what I can
do then." Robert Lowe took a sounder
view of the position. " It is," he said,
" the business of the Chancellor of the
Exchequer to distribute a certain amount
of human misery; and the man who dis-
tributes it most equally is the best Chancellor." Mr. Bonar Law is, I believe, very
much of the same opinion as his less
popular predecessor, and he is certainly

162

distributing the misery with lavish hand. Whether he has yet succeeded in attaining equality I am not quite sure. In spite of the super-tax, the man with £50,000 a year still seems appreciably more comfortable than the man with £500 a year. To the last-named sufferer it is quite needless for Cabinet Ministers and Bishops and Judges to preach thrift. It is preached by the still more persuasive voices of the Tax-gatherer and the Rate-collector. He reduces his expenditure because he has less to spend. " Haven't you got any old clothes? " exclaims the energetic lady who runs the Red Cross Hospital. " Have I any others? " he replies. " If you t⁻' my old clothes, I must lie in bed till the war is over."

In the wide intervening region between £500 a year and £50,000, thrift is practised on voluntary principles ; and the greater the house the more conspicuous the change produced by War-Economy. The *chef* is fighting for France ; the footmen are fighting for England. The butler is obviously beyond military age; and his grandson, who officiates as valet and groom-of-the-chambers, has apparently just escaped from the Elementary School.

V

CHIVALRY

THE word which heads this chapter stands
for an Ideal. Certainly that ideal has
been from time to time encrusted by
accretions which obscured its true character. It has been associated with a
vainglorious militarism, with the servile
subordination of class to class, with the
darkness and violence of mediæval Europe.
Even Burke, its most impassioned champion, mixed the good and the evil which
the word suggests, in undiscriminating
eulogy :—

Never, never more, shall we behold that generous
loyalty to rank and sex, that proud submission, that
dignified obedience, that subordination of the heart,
which kept alive, even in servitude itself, the spirit of
an exalted freedom ! The unbought grace of life,
the cheap defence of nations, the nurse of manly
sentiment and heroic enterprise, is gone ! It is gone

that sensibility of principle, that chastity of honour, which felt a stain like a wound, which inspired courage while it mitigated ferocity, which ennobled whatever it touched, and under which vice itself lost half its evil by losing all its grossness !

That last clause is ethically unsound, and in the preceding exclamations the good and the evil of chivalry are strangely confused ; but these are the faults of exuberance, and Burke touched the heart of the matter when he said that, if chivalry is renounced, " a woman is but an animal, and an animal not of the highest order. All homage paid to the sex in general as such, and without distinct views, is to be regarded as romance and folly."

The true ideal — the inner spirit — of chivalry was the championship of the weak by the strong. In a special, though not an exclusive, sense chivalry meant the protection of womankind from injury and insult. To the chivalrous heart, and, if need were, to the chivalrous sword, no woman could appeal in vain.

166

CHIVALRY

As we look back to the Middle Age, we seem to see nothing but a welter of bloodshed and devastation :—

The heavens all gloom, the wearied earth all crime.

But from the dead-level of violent wrong which fills the centuries there emerge, at intervals, higher points of horror, and one of these is, and always has been, the murder of the Maid of Orleans. " A national instead of a party cry, strict morality enforced by a Heaven-sent virgin, and the enthusiasm of religion," were the aids which she brought to the service of her country ; and her reward was death by fire. All that was chivalrous in human nature revolted from the deed and enrolled Joan of Arc, by a kind of informal canonization, in the Kalendar of Saints. We leave the Middle Age behind and embark on the new world. Chivalry is not dead, though, as before and since, it is overcome by brutal and calculated violence. Mary Queen of Scots is justly chargeable with real and grievous crimes.

167

POLITICS AND PERSONALITIES

If she had died a natural death, even though
it were at Loch Leven or at Fotheringay,
the world in general would have been as
hard on her memory as Froude himself.
But the very fact that a defeated and
friendless woman perished by the execu-
tioner's axe rallied affection and forgiveness
to her side.

" Judge Jeffreys " is a name which, for
two centuries, has borne much the same
significance in English jurisprudence as
Pontius Pilate in the Creed. It has stood
for judicial murder inflicted in the name
of law, and for the effusion of innocent
blood. Yet even in that hideous record
there stands one act which English chivalry
has always remembered with peculiar loath-
ing. At Jeffreys' bidding a woman was
beheaded because she had given " a morsel
of bread and a cup of water to a hunted
rebel " ; and as long as men remember
Jeffreys they will remember Alice Lisle.

The French Revolution was, in its origin,
an expiation of intolerable wrongs ; and
England might well have stood on one

side while a sister-country was readjusting her social order, even though by rough methods. But, when Marie Antoinette died by the guillotine, it did not need Burke's eloquence to rouse the chivalry of England. We went into the French war as into a crusade, and forgot all the crimes of the Kings of France in compassion for a butchered Queen, and for the long train of brave and innocent women who followed her to the scaffold.

When England learned that Nana Sahib had hacked to death the English ladies whom he had imprisoned, then—and not till then—Englishmen were stirred to deeds of just though frightful retribution. Macaulay wrote : " I who cannot bear to see a beast or bird in pain, could look on without winking while Nana Sahib underwent all the torments of Ravaillac." Oliver Wendell Holmes, surveying from neutral ground the crime and the punishment, said : " England takes down the Map of the World, which she has girdled with empire, and makes a correction thus :

DELHI, *Dele*. The civilized world says, ' Amen ! ' "

We look back ; we look round us ; we look forward. The aspect of Europe in the Middle Age was scarcely more horrible or more threatening than its aspect in the Twentieth Century. Rapine and bloodshed are only more scientific now than then, and human savagery, bursting through the thin veneer of civilization, shows no trace of diminution. Yet, even over the horrors which have surrounded us for the last three years, certain incidents tower in a hateful eminence ; and of those incidents the most loathsome is, again, the murder of a woman.

The age of chivalry, said Burke, is gone ; but he despaired too soon. Its outward forms and trappings, its speech and its methods, have changed with the changing world ; but its inner spirit lives, and will live as long as any spark of the Divine nature dwells in the hearts of men. Chivalry is the defence of the weak by the strong. Chivalry is the service which every man owes to every woman. Death is not the deepest injury which womankind can suffer, nor the only enemy against which man is bound to protect her. Let every Englishman whose blood boils with impotent rage when he thinks of Edith Cavell's execution bind himself by a Crusader's vow that, though he could not save her life, he will do what in him lies to save the honour of her sisters in the human family. Then, as Lincoln resolved that, from the cemetery of Gettysburg, America should have "a new birth of freedom," so, from the grave where Edith Cavell lies, England shall have a new birth of that manly virtue which is the very soul of Chivalry.

VI

THE DARK SIDE OF SCIENCE

My title sounds like a parody. The gifted Mrs. Crowe thrilled the young people of her time with *The Night Side of Nature*, and perhaps some echo of those mysterious words flitted across my mind when I read Professor Osler's remarkable lecture on the horrors which Science has added to war :—

It has made slaughter possible on a scale never dreamt of before, and it has enormously increased man's capacity to maim and to disable his fellow-men.

When I was a boy, "Science" was entering on a triumphant period of its career, and the word had lately come to bear a new and an exclusive sense. "Science" at Oxford had always meant moral and mental science—ethic, logic, and, within bounds, metaphysic. "We elected

172

him for his science," said the Principal of Brasenose about Walter Pater, who had just got his Fellowship, and certainly knew no more of electricity or physiology than I know of space. Elsewhere the word "Science" was commonly used with a descriptive epithet, and men spoke of moral science or mental science or physical science, thereby relating the word to one or other of the three parts which were then held to constitute the man.

But about 1860 a curious change came over common speech, and men who talked of Science were found to mean, exclusively, physical or natural science— the science which deals with material phenomena. There were reasons for the change. Moral science had sunk into disfavour, and was branded as an anachronism or a superstition by those who held that man has no means of establishing a relation with God, and that there is, therefore, no absolute standard of right and wrong. Mental science had been discredited by the dogmatism of those who most strenuously upheld it, and most scornfully rejected moral science. Mr. Balfour has admirably shown, in an autobiographical passage of his " Lectures on Theism and Humanism," that such teachers as Mill and Leslie Stephen drove some enquiring minds in the exactly opposite direction to that which they intended. Moral and mental science having both receded, natural or physical science acquired the exclusive right to the title of " Science." The physicists took the concrete world as they found it, they investigated it, and they utilized it. They cared not a jot for the Platonists who said that stones and plants and animals were not realities, but only ideas. They would have sympathized with Sydney Smith, who, sending a brace of grouse to a metaphysical friend, said : " In other and better language, they are mere ideas, shot by other ideas, out of a purely intellectual notion called a gun." They thought, and they made others think, that in confining their attention to the natural world they

174

had got down to reality. Theologians might harangue about right and wrong, and philosophers might argue interminably about the nature of knowledge ; but a man who worked at chemistry or botany or anatomy, had got hold of something definite, and showed results from his labours which none could gainsay.

And Science, in this restricted sense, had a great deal to say for itself. Not every one thinks, but every one feels ; and each person who sent a telegram, or travelled on a railway, or took an anæsthetic, felt that life had been made perceptibly more comfortable by Science. So Science had its heyday. Every schoolboy must be taught it. Every one who pretended to culture must be able to chatter about it. Plausible M.P.'s must lecture on it to their constituents. Popular clergymen must preach about it—either against it, as an invention of the Evil One, or for it, as a revelation of the Divine. The heyday of Science was also the heyday of materialism. The facts of spiritual experience were ignored or denied, and the disputations of the philosophers interested no one outside the Universities. Material prosperity was abundant. Wealth was increasing rapidly. The comforts and conveniences and luxuries of life were multiplied beyond all precedent ; and every one said that these were the blessed results of Science. Every fresh discovery of the forces latent in nature was hailed as in itself a good. But just in the middle of this triumphant period, which I date from 1860 to 1880, a warning voice was heard. In 1870 Ruskin delivered his inaugural lecture as Slade Professor at Oxford, and thus addressed his undergraduate hearers :—

Within the last few years we have had the laws of natural science opened to us with a rapidity which has been blinding by its brightness ; and means of transit and communication given to us, which have made but one kingdom of the habitable globe. One kingdom ;—but who is to be its king? Is there to be no king in it, think you, and every man to do that which is right in his own eyes? Or only kings of terror, and the obscene empires of Mammon and Belial?

THE DARK SIDE OF SCIENCE

The words were prophetic. Within six months the Franco-Prussian War had broken out, and " Science " had shown the world what it could do in the artistic destruction of human life on a scale then unprecedented. But England did not pause to ponder the lesson, and for another ten years Science pursued its triumphant way, acclaimed on all hands as the one subject worthy of human study. From a point which we may roughly date about 1880, finer voices began to make themselves heard. Men appeared, quite outside the ranks of professional theologians, who taught that the things of the spirit are, after all, the things that really matter ; that the moral life is quite as interesting as the bodily life, and more important, as it lasts considerably longer. In brief, the spiritual idea of the world arrayed itself once more against the material idea, and the ups and downs of that struggle form the philosophical history of 1880-1914. Then, swift and terrible as the lightning of God, came the vindication of the spiritual contention. All at once the world saw, and has from that time continued to see, what Science can effect for human misery—

In the making of 15-inch guns, that will throw with accuracy a ton of metal a dozen or more miles, is found such a combination of brains and machinery as does not exist in any other human product.

To guns, add submarines and Zeppelins and poisonous gases, and yet you have not half exhausted the devilries of which Science is capable.

It is true that Professor Osler goes on to show the alleviating effects of Science in medicine and surgery, and these no moralist would deny or belittle. But the conclusion of the whole matter is that Science is not, as its devotees fifty years ago believed, a good in itself. It is merely power ; and whether it is a blessing or a curse to the world depends entirely on the spirit in which, and the objects for which, it is employed. Even Science is a smaller thing than the human will.

VII

WATERLOO

IF the Centenary of Waterloo had fallen
in a normal year it might, I fear, have
been celebrated by an outbreak of offensive Jingoism. Our fire-eaters of Press
and platform would scarcely have been
content to glorify that supreme performance of British arms without some disparagement of the nation which we then
defeated. The opponents of free institutions
would probably have used the occasion for
an attack, more or less decently veiled,
on French Republicanism, and would have
urged the duty of closer relations with
that military despotism which inherits the
traditions of Blücher. A centenary of
Waterloo, dominated by such influences as
these, would have been a triumph of bad
taste and bad feeling. But now all is

179

changed. We have seen in practice what we have long believed in theory about the character and fruits of militarism. We have found in Republican and industrial France our gallant and cordial ally; and, if we refer to the great event of a hundred years ago, we speak in no spirit of vulgar boastfulness. We are thankful for deliverance from a danger even more formidable than that which threatens us to-day, but we recognize as amply as the French themselves the genius which then so nearly subjugated us. We rejoice that the descendants of the men who fought against us in 1815 are in 1915 fighting with us for freedom and civilization.

The accidents of life linked me, in early youth, with survivors of the Napoleonic period, and another such link recurs to my mind to-day. I do not propose to re-open the much-controverted question of the particular spot in " Belgium's capital " on which the Duchess of Richmond gave her ball and awoke the " sound of revelry by night "; but it interests me to remem-

180

ber that two of her daughters, with whom, as the Scotch say, I "called cousins," survived into the present century, and that the one whom I knew best was brought down from her nursery-bed to buckle the Duke of Wellington's sword as he set out from the ball-room on his way to Quatre Bras.

In *The Spirit of England* I described the doings of "The Hundred Days," when Englishmen, who had fondly believed that Napoleon would remain quietly at Elba for the remainder of his natural life, discovered, to their great astonishment, that he had escaped from that enforced seclusion, and was marching triumphantly towards Paris. The newly-restored King fled at his approach. Evidently a conclusive struggle was now at hand, and the Allied Powers of Europe agreed that Wellington was the one man in whom Napoleon might find his match. But Wellington, whose caution was a form of genius, and who, in his own phrase, had "spent his life in guessing what was on

181

the other side of the hill," was in no
hurry to begin. He knew that England
was not prepared for the fight, and he
resolved to postpone the opening of the campaign till June or July. On the 10th of May,
1815, William Wilberforce wrote in his
diary: "If Bonaparte could be unhorsed
it would, humanly speaking, be a blessing to the European world, indeed to all
nations, and Government ought to know
both his force and their own. Yet I
greatly dread their being deceived, remembering how Pitt was." On the 15th:
"All this time, a fearful interval, expect-
ing the bursting out of the war. It is
amazing how little people seem moved."
The 18th of June was a Sunday—"that
loud Sabbath " which Tennyson extolled
in later years. Wilberforce spent it
quietly at Taplow Vicarage. "Perhaps,"
he said to his children on the way to
church—" perhaps at this very moment,
when we are walking thus in peace
together to the house of God, our brave
fellows may be fighting hard in Belgium."
182

On the 22nd he knew that he had divined aright. "A dreadful battle," he writes. "British victorious, but great loss. We are said to have lost twenty-five thousand men, the French fifty thousand. Oh! my heart sickens at the scene! Yet, praise God for this wonderful victory." It all reads like a narrative of the present day, reduced in scale, but animated by exactly the same spirit; and the similarity is completed by these last entries :—" Took the chair at a meeting of neighbours for a fund for the widows and children of the killed and wounded belonging to the 1st Life Guards, always quartered at Knightsbridge." " I never see a soldier or a sailor without a mingled feeling of gratitude and compassion."

The first person in England to receive the news of Waterloo was Nathan Meyer Rothschild, who had recently settled in London, and laid the foundations of the great business which still bears his name. A messenger, some say a member, of the firm had crossed the Channel in

an open boat, and brought some information which suggested a large and
profitable investment in Consols. That
stroke of business accomplished, the
emissary was sent to the Prime Minister,
Lord Liverpool, and had considerable
difficulty in persuading him that the good
news was true. So, not for the last time,
Finance outran Statesmanship in the attainment of knowledge which changed the face
of Europe.

How had the victory been won? By
good luck or good guidance? By fortune
or genius? Military historians of all
countries have contested every inch of this
ground, with very different results. An
audacious attempt by Mrs. Arbuthnot, wife
of the Duke's Private Secretary, to elicit
the Duke's own opinion on the question,
fared as it deserved :—" You won't mind
telling me, Duke, for we are such old
friends—is it true that you were surprised
at Waterloo?" "By G——, mum, not half
as much surprised as I am now!"

The great majority of Englishmen have

184

accepted the Duke's own declaration that throughout that long day of struggle he never was alarmed about the result; and have agreed to believe, with his arch-toady, Wilson Croker, in " the clear lucidity of a mind that rose high above the clouds of battle accumulated below." So perhaps it was. I do not pretend to an opinion, for the civilian critic of military operations courts discomfiture. He fails, not because he lacks the necessary information—for that can be acquired—but because, where the instinct of war is lacking, the greater the information, the greater the confusion. The final word on Waterloo was uttered by the Duke in private conversation nineteen years after the event—" Waterloo did more than any other battle I know of towards the true object of all battles—the peace of the world."

The words deserve all the emphasis which we can give. The " Hero of a Hundred Fights " tells us that the true object of all battles is the peace of the world.

185

POLITICS AND PERSONALITIES

Here is the warrant for the work in which
England and France are now engaged;
and here is the issue for which we strive
and pray.

VIII

GREECE

IT requires some courage in these troublous
times to declare oneself an impenitent Phil-
Hellene. Yet that is my confession, and
I will try to justify it. I hold that
one's debt to a country or a race which
has rendered conspicuous service to the
world is inextinguishable, and from that
point of view the Greeks are " of earth's
first blood, have titles manifold." Greece
gave the modern world its intellect ; and
it was truly said by Gladstone that " the
place of Aristotle and Plato in Christian
education is not arbitrary, nor in principle
mutable." Our modern psychology dates
itself back to its origin in Aristotelian
classification. The Platonic way of eliciting truth, by questioning and doubt and
irony, has been the age-long foe of rash
dogmatism ; and to the author of the

Phædo, more conspicuously than to any other thinker of the ancient world, it was given to anticipate the revelation of a personal immortality. The life of the Greek Republics brought out into vivid consciousness the idea of free and honourable citizenship. Greek art fixed the forms of beauty for all time.

Deep, then, is our debt to Greece on the intellectual side; and on the religious side it is deeper still. From the day when the black hoof of the Turkish invader first ravaged the fairest provinces of Christendom, to a date within the recollection of people still alive, the Greeks were martyrs and confessors for the cause of Christ; and, through centuries of bodily and moral torture, they bore their irrefragable testimony to the Religion of the Cross. For that testimony, if for nothing else, our nominally Christian Europe owes Greece an imperishable debt.

In all ages and all countries the twin-spirits of Liberty and Patriotism have

188

found their natural vent in lyrical poetry ;
and Greece, rich in lyrics of her own, has
had a singular power of eliciting the
" lyrical cry " from others. If England
is glorious by anything, she is glorious
by her poetry, and among her poets Byron
stands eminent. In his character there
is much to distress, and even to disgust ;
but the inspiration of Greece raised his
genius to its highest flights, and awoke
whatever was chivalrous and heroic in his
strangely mingled nature. Byron died for
Greece, and by so dying he bound the
two countries together with a bond which
may be strained, but never can be broken.
But then, as now, Phil-Hellenism was an
unpopular creed. The claims of the intellect and the spirit appealed in vain to
the type of mind which admires nothing
but size and force and material prosperity.
Sir James Mackintosh had critics of this
type in view when, in 1823, he delivered
his famous oration :—

If we rest the claims of the Greeks on the interests
of Liberty, they call it revolutionary rant. If we

speak of the interests of Religion, they call it the cant of fanaticism. If we give utterance to the sentiments which we are bound to cherish for the great teachers, instructors and ornaments of mankind, they deride us for using the commonplaces of schoolboys.

At the moment Mackintosh seemed to speak in vain, but four years later England, Russia, and France shared the glory of Navarino; and it was the English admiral who struck the decisive blow.

All these heroic memories, stretching back to the fourth century before the Christian era, and ranging from Marathon to Missolonghi, were revived for Englishmen by the Græco-Turkish war of 1897. That war, and the Armenian atrocities out of which it sprang, stirred the chivalry of young England as it had not been stirred since the days of Garibaldi and the Thousand. A Phil-Hellenic Legion, defying or evading all the restrictions imposed by international law, formed itself in London, and went off to the campaign in Greece in the same spirit as animated our crusading forefathers. One of the

19c

noblest lives that England gave to Greece was that of Clement Harris, who counted ease and wealth, and even the art which he so dearly loved, as naught when faith and freedom demanded sacrifice. On the 5th of April, 1897, he made this entry in his diary :—

I am off this afternoon to Arta to enlist in the Greek Army. . . . I have not time to write much this morning, but I only wish it to be clearly understood that no one is responsible in the least degree for the step which I have taken, and which to many may appear as an act of madness, but to myself (who have given the matter the fullest consideration) the least a man of honour can perform towards a country which crying for liberty in the name of the Cross, has been insulted and threatened by each so-called civilized Power successively. Unfortunately, I have not time to explain myself more clearly—but lovers of freedom will recognize a deeper motive for my thus offering myself to the service of a distressed and misunderstood country.

Three weeks later he fell at the battle of Pentepigadia, and no one knows the place of his sepulchre unto this day.

In that stirring and chivalrous time I was closely associated with many who risked their lives for Greece, and none of them, as far as I know, have ever repented of the venture. But from their concurrent testimony I derived a very strong impression that, as an ancient poet of Greece once said, " There are many who bear the reed, but few true bacchanals." There were professed and ostensible Greeks, sometimes in important stations, who had neither Hellenic blood in their veins nor Hellenic sympathies in their hearts. This fact co-operated with the poltroonery which at that time governed English politics, and with that " mutual distrust and hatred of the European Powers " which was Gladstone's synonym for the Concert of Europe. The most beautiful woman I ever saw was a Greek, and when I was introduced to her she asked if I had ever seen a Greek before. I replied that I was acquainted with this or that Greek family, but she replied, with a disdainful smile : " Greeks ! Do they look like it ? They are Levantines. My blood is unmixed." And certainly she looked as if Pheidias would have loved

192

to immortalize her in marble or Apelles on canvas. She was Greek to the core, and she came from the mountains, where Freedom has ever loved to dwell. Let us bear in mind that Athens is not Greece.

Another report in which my friends returning from the campaign were unanimous was that Greece was tired of an alien monarchy, and was ripe for a republic. I know that circumstances have changed, and that a king born and bred in Greece may have a stronger hold on his people than any of his imported predecessors. But the Poets are the Prophets, and Byron's prophecy may yet be verified in the land for which he died : " The King-times," he said, " are fast finishing ; there will be blood shed like water and tears like mist, but the peoples will conquer in the end. I shall not live to see it ; but I foresee it."

III

PERSONALITIES
ANCIENT AND MODERN

I

A QUEEN READY-MADE

LORD ESHER'S name is a synonym for discretion.[1] When, therefore, this adroit and trusty courtier tells us that Princess Victoria was not warmly attached to her mother, and detested her mother's surroundings ; that she was not highly educated ; that she was by nature " auto-cratic " and " not very tender " ; and that she " avoided intimacies with members of her household " ; and when, quite incidentally, he informs us that the King's " dream " is to pull down Buckingham Palace and transfer the Court to Kensington, we may be sure that he is speak-

[1] *The Girlhood of Queen Victoria : a Selection from Her Majesty's Diaries between the years 1832 and 1840.* Edited by Viscount Esher.

197

ing with the full concurrence of the Illustrious Personages who have supervised his labours. Lord Esher does not write at random. That curious remark about Buckingham Palace may be thrown out for the guidance of some future Commissioner of Works ; and the care with which he notes Queen Victoria's limitations may be designed to show that, though a courtier, he retains the right of private judgment.

The Queen began to keep a journal when she was thirteen, and before she died it filled over a hundred volumes. The first entry is dated Wednesday, August 1, 1832 ; and Lord Esher reminds us that the journal was not a sealed book :—
" It was not privately put away under lock and key, and reserved only for the eye of the writer. The young Princess's journal was commenced in a volume given to her by her mother, for the express purpose that she should record the facts of her daily life, and that this record of facts and impressions should be open
198

to the inspection of the child's governess as well as of her mother." A record exposed to this twofold censorship would naturally be discreet, and anything which it may have lacked in that direction is supplied by the scrupulous care of Lord Esher. Asterisks, though virtuous, are always tantalizing.

It appears that in the domestic circle Princess Victoria habitually spoke German, with interludes of French; and the fact that English was not her earliest language manifests itself in various breaches of the English idiom. " Who " appears where " whom " should be. " Led Mamma and I " is not good. " I had not seen him since four years," and " The news of the King are worse," betray a foreign influence. The ordinary Briton finds it difficult to write a long letter in the third person, so we need not be too critical of this reference to Sir Robert Peel : " The Queen don't like his manner. . . . The Duke I like far better than Peel. The Queen trusts that Lord Melbourne will excuse this long letter." It used to be a tradition of good English that one never "took" anything except exercise and physic ; but Princess Victoria "took" breakfast, dinner, coffee, and tea. It is surprising to find that she used the hideous but convenient modernism, "We lunched "; though happily she avoided the truncated substantive from which that base verb is derived. On the other hand, she retained some forms of speech which were already obsolescent. Sir George Trevelyan has told us that Macaulay never would allow his nieces to say : "The tea is being made," but insisted on "The tea is making." Lord Russell once convened a meeting of his party in Chesham Place, because "Glad-stone's house was painting"; and Princess Victoria, agreeably to this antique usage, "read *The Conquest of Granada* while my hair was doing," and "read in Shakespeare while my hair was undoing." There is a pleasant sound of old times in "well beat," and "ill-written," and "sung" as the perfect of sing, and "play-house" for

200

theatre ; but a room " giving on the park " sounds rather American than English.

Yet although there were these traces of foreign influence in the young Princess's style, there were none in her character or conduct. It would be difficult to depict a nature more entirely English in its likes and dislikes, its prejudices and predilections. She had flawless health and inexhaustible energy ; she loved concerts and theatres, dancing and riding, regattas and races and reviews ; delighted in her pet dogs, and birds, and horses, and enumerated even her smallest presents on Christmas Days and birthdays, with all the zest of youthful ownership.

Princess Victoria had now struck sixteen, and she knew that, if she lived, in two years' time she would be old enough to reign. She wrote in her journal for the 24th of May, 1835 :—" I feel that the two years to come, till I attain my eighteenth birthday, are the most important of almost any." A year later she wrote about the death of her old nurse :—" My chief regret is

that she did not live till I was my own
mistress, and could make her quite comfortable " ; and, having made great friends
with a family of gipsies encamped near
Claremont—" such a nice set of gipsies, so
quiet, so affectionate to one another, so
discreet "—she recorded a generous aspiration :—" I trust in Heaven that the day
may come when I may do something for
these poor people, and for this particular
family. . . . Whenever any poor gipsies are
encamped anywhere, and crimes and robberies
should occur, it is invariably laid to their
account, which is shocking ; and, if they
are always looked upon as vagabonds, how
can they become good people ? . . . The
gipsy family, Cooper, will *never* be obliterated
from my memory ! "

And now the eventful day drew on,
which would bring the Heiress Presump-
tive to her legal majority. Here I pause
to justify my title. Such are the tricks
of language that, if I had written " A
Ready-made Queen," the phrase would have
had a derogatory and cheapening sound;

but the transposition of the substantive and the epithet exactly conveys my meaning. William IV was nearing his end, and his successor was "ready-made"—prepared in advance for the fulfilment of her unique and astonishing destiny. Her uncle, King Leopold (of whom Lord Esher says that he thought he had reduced the rules of sovereignty to a science), was *il mio secondo padre*, or rather *solo padre*; and he employed the mysterious Stockmar, a physician turned diplomatist, to inculcate what he esteemed wholesome lessons. The Princess had met the principal statesmen of the day at her mother's dinner-table, but "there is nothing in the journals or elsewhere to show that before she was eighteen she had ever talked seriously or at any length to any man or woman of exceptional gifts."

Early in May 1837 it became known that the King was dangerously ill. The flutter of excitement, the hum of rumours, contradictions, and explanations, to which the news gave rise, are described by a

master-hand in the sixth chapter of *Sybil*. On
the 13th of June Lord Melbourne instructed
Greville, as Clerk of the Council, to " get
everything ready quietly " for the Council
which must be held on the accession.
On the 15th the Princess wrote in her
journal : " I just hear that the doctors
think my poor uncle the King cannot last
more than forty-eight hours ! Poor man !
He was always kind to me, and he *meant*
it well, I know ; I am grateful for it,
and shall ever remember his kindness with
gratitude. He was odd, very odd and
singular, but his intentions were often ill-
interpreted."

In the early dawn of June 20, Archbishop Howley and the Lord Chamberlain,
Lord Conygham, galloped up from Windsor
as fast as four horses could bring them,
and made their way, after considerable
difficulties with sentries and porters, into
the Palace. Here the journal must be
resumed :—" I was woke at six o'clock
by Mamma, who told me that the Archbishop of Canterbury and Lord Conygham

were here, and wished to see me. I got out of bed and went into my sitting-room (only in my dressing-gown), and *alone*, and saw them. Lord Conygham (the Lord Chamberlain) then acquainted me that my poor uncle, the King, was no more, and had expired at twelve minutes p. two this morning, and consequently that I am *Queen*. Lord Conygham knelt down and kissed my hand, at the same time delivering to me the official announcement of the poor King's demise. . . . Lord Conygham, whom I charged to express my feelings of condolence and sorrow to the poor Queen, returned directly to Windsor. I then went to my room and dressed.

" Since it has pleased Providence to place me in this station, I shall do my utmost to fulfil my duty towards my country. I am very young, and perhaps in many, though not in all, things inexperienced ; but I am sure that very few have more real goodwill and more real desire to do what is fit and right than I have."

It is impossible to transcribe these words

without astonishment at the fortitude of a girl, barely out of the schoolroom, who mounts a throne—and such a throne !—with this absolute composure. The journal proceeds :—

> Breakfasted. . . . At nine came Lord Melbourne whom I saw in my room, and, of COURSE, *quite* ALONE, as I shall *always* do all my Ministers. He kissed my hand and I then acquainted him that it had long been my intention to retain him and the rest of the present Ministry at the head of affairs, and that it could not be in better hands than his.

" *Long* "—and the young lady had not been for quite two months of an age to exercise her sovereignty !

At noon she was presiding at her first Council, and the Duke of Wellington affirmed that " if she had been his own daughter, he could not have desired to see her perform her part better." Next day she was proclaimed, and held a second Council, " at which she presided with as much ease as if she had been doing nothing else all her life." And so began an exercise of queenship which endured with ever-increasing influence over public affairs till the autumn of 1900.

These journals are delightfully human in their pictures of life and its enjoyments; and they convey a very strong sense of that absolute straightforwardness with which their writer was always credited by those who knew her best. "Lehzen," she said, referring to her old governess, "Lehzen often said that she had never seen such a passionate and naughty child as I was; but I had never told a falsehood, though I knew I should be punished." The days of punishment were now over, and the emancipated Princess enjoyed herself to the top of her bent.

It is the tritest commonplace to say that Queen Victoria owed much to Lord Melbourne; but these journals show that she owed him even more than we knew, and perhaps in rather unexpected ways. That he was her sedulous and sagacious counsellor in her principles and working of the Constitution we all knew; and it is interesting to note that his counsels

became more and more authoritative as
months went by. But, apart from these
political lessons, the Queen soon fell into
the habit of jotting down fragments from
Melbourne's table-talk ; and these fragments convey some sense of the bracing
and widening effect of his mind on hers.
His view of life generally was informal,
individual, unconventional ; and his conversation was enlivened by those touches
of paradox which are useful in making
young people think. For a girl reared
in the cloister-like seclusion of Kensington Palace, taught by a Dean, a Duchess,
and an Old Maid, and never allowed to
read a novel, it must have been an instructive experience to hear Melbourne
discoursing on horses and dogs and
women's beauty, on the gossip of the
eighteenth century, on the excellence of
pensions, on the crimes of navvies, on
the tiresomeness of education, on the virtues
of Euthanasia, on the foolishness of the
Irbys, on the merits and defects of Eton,
on Shakespeare and Scott, and English

208

pronunciation and French cooking, and
snoring in church, and conjugal relationships ; " —— was separated from her husband, and excited pity, as he was known
or supposed to have beat her. Upon this
Lord Melbourne said : ' Why, it is almost
worth while for a woman to be beat,
considering the exceeding pity she excites,'
which made us laugh."

The Queen had come to the throne,
" ready-made " as far as knowledge of the
rights and duties of the Crown was concerned, and not without preferences as
between political parties. Two years after
her accession she wrote : " I had been
always brought up in very strong feelings
on the Whig side " ; and Melbourne's influence naturally confirmed those feelings.
Very soon the Queen identified herself with
her Ministers in a degree which certainly
was not repeated until Lord Beaconsfield's
second Administration. She watched the
Elections with anxious interest ; was delighted when Whigs were returned, and
thankful when Tories or Radicals were

o

defeated. A bad division in the House
of Commons affected her like a personal
calamity :—

> May 7th, 1839.—I awoke at ½ p. 8 and heard from
> Lord Surrey that we had only had a majority of
> five! This struck to my heart, and I felt dreadfully
> anxious. . . . I received a letter from Lord Melbourne,
> in which he stated what had taken place, that he had
> not yet heard from Lord John, but that he feared they
> had no other alternative—*can I write it ?*—but to resign.

This extract refers to a crisis which,
though in some of its bearings serious
enough, yet in others wore the semblance
of a Comedy of Errors. For an account
of it I turn from Lord Esher to Lord
Beaconsfield :—" One morning there was an
odd whisper in the circle of first initia-
tion. The clubs were crowded, even at
noon. Everywhere a mysterious bustle and
an awful stir. What could be the matter?
What had happened? The world was
employed the whole of the morning in
asking and answering this important question, ' Is it true?' Towards dinner-time
it was settled universally in the affirma-

tive ; and then the world went out to dine and to ascertain why it was true and how it was true.

"And now, what had really happened? What had happened was what is commonly called a ' hitch.' The Whig Ministers, it seemed, had resigned ; but somehow or other had not entirely and completely gone out. What a constitutional dilemma ! But then the oddest rumour in the world got about. . . . It seemed, though, of course, no one could for a moment credit it, that these rebellious, wrong-headed Ministers, who would not go out, wore petticoats ! "

In plainer phrase, Lord Melbourne and his colleagues had obtained a majority of only five on a Bill to suspend the Constitution of Jamaica, "a measure requiring more than ordinary support and confidence, but which had met with less than was usually accorded to them." This rebuff they treated as a Vote of Want of Confidence, and determined to resign. When Melbourne placed the resignation in the Queen's hands, she "held his hand for

a little while, unable to let go," and said,
" You will not forsake me." Lord John
Russell, as Leader of the House of Commons, came to explain the case, and thanked
the Queen for her kindness, " which quite
set me off crying, and I said it was a
terrible thing for me." Later in the day
Melbourne returned, " having written down
what he thought the Queen should do."
The conclusion of the paper was : " Your
Majesty had better express your hope that
none of Your Majesty's Household, except
those who are engaged in politics, may
be removed." This done, the Queen summoned the Duke of Wellington, as titular
Leader of the victorious party, Melbourne
good-naturedly smoothing the way by saying that the Duke was very deaf—" Mind
the Duke understands what you say." The
Duke came, and " was kind " ; and on
his advice the Queen summoned Sir Robert
Peel, whose strategy had defeated the
Government. What then ensued is best
given in the Queen's words :—" The Queen
repeated what she had said to the Duke

212

about her former Government, and asked
Sir Robert to form a new Ministry. He
does not seem sanguine ; says entering on
the Government in a minority is very
difficult. . . . He felt the task arduous,
and that he would require me to demon-
strate (a *certain* degree, if any, I can
only feel) confidence in the Government,
and that my Household would be one of
the marks of that. The Queen mentioned
the same thing about the Household, to
which he at present would give no answer,
but said nothing should be done without
my knowledge or approbation. . . . He is
such a cold, odd man. She can't make
out what he means. . . . The Queen was
very much collected, civil, and high, and
betrayed no agitation during these two trying Audiences. But afterwards, again, *all*
gave way." What Peel meant was disclosed in an Audience on the 9th of May,
which Her Majesty thus described in a letter
to Melbourne :—

Sir Robert has behaved very ill. He insisted on
my giving up my ladies, to which I replied that I

never would consent, and I never saw a man so frightened ; he said he must go to the Duke of Wellington and consult with him. . . . I was calm, but very decided ; and I think you would have been pleased to see my composure and great firmness. The Queen of England will not submit to such trickery. Keep yourself in readiness, for you may soon be wanted.

Later in the day Peel came again, urged the dismissal of the Ladies, and was told that the Queen would " reflect, but felt certain she should not change her mind." Then came Melbourne, and " approved all, and said I could not do otherwise. I acted quite alone, I said, and feared I might have embarrassed the Government. ' I must summon the Cabinet,' said Lord M., ' at once ; it may have very serious consequences.' "

The Cabinet met, deliberated, and recommended the Queen to write as follows to Peel :—

The Queen, having considered the proposal made to her yesterday by Sir Robert Peel to remove the Ladies of her Bedchamber, cannot consent to adopt a course which she conceives to be contrary to usage and which is repugnant to her feelings.

214

On receipt of this very clear decision, Peel declined the task of forming an Administration, and Melbourne and his colleagues resumed the offices which they had not technically vacated.

Disraeli, in *Sybil*, trounced the Conservative Leader for his maladroit dealings with a young and impressionable Sovereign, and ridiculed the policy which had been " brained by a fan." Charles Greville wrote : " It is a high trial to our institutions when the wishes of a Princess of nineteen can overturn a great Ministerial combination." Lord Esher tells us that the Queen, in her old age, said : " I was very young then, and perhaps I should act differently if it was all to be done again " ; and that Melbourne blamed himself in after years for not having warned the Queen of the changes which Peel might demand ; but this self-reproach seems unnecessary in view of the Queen's words quoted above. Whether Peel ever repented of his share in the transaction is extremely doubtful. It was all very well

215

for Disraeli, who had hoped for some modest preferment under Peel's Administration, to say that "the Leader of the Tory Party should have vindicated his natural position, and availed himself of the gracious occasion. He missed it, and the Whigs enjoyed its occurrence." But probably when, two years later, Peel became Prime Minister, at the head of a triumphant majority and with a conciliated Court, he was glad that he had not clutched the Premiership at a moment when neither Queen nor Commons wished him well.

The "Bedchamber Plot" of 1839 was the last event of political importance which these volumes record, for on the 15th of October, 1839, the Queen proposed to Prince Albert, and the remainder of the narrative is a smooth tale of love.

II

AN UNCROWNED KING

THIRTY-FIVE years ago the great Lord
Shaftesbury told me what was then a piece
of secret history. He said that Queen Victoria had been very anxious that the title
of King-Consort should be conferred on
Prince Albert, and that, as this could only
be done by Act of Parliament, she had
repeatedly urged Lord Melbourne to bring
in a Bill conferring the title. Melbourne
demurred ; the Queen persisted ; and then
the sagacious statesman gave the necessary
warning :—" For G——'s sake, Ma'am, let's
hear no more of it. If you once get the
English people into the way of making
Kings, they'll learn the way of unmaking
them." This Lord Shaftesbury had direct
from Melbourne (who was Lady Shaftesbury's uncle), and Memoirs published under

217

Royal authority in recent years have proved
it to be true.

But the refusal of the Crown Matri-
monial made no difference to the actual
power of Prince Albert, though much to
his seeming dignity. He was a man of
high intelligence, assiduously cultivated. He
devoted himself to the study of constitutional and international law. He watched
every turn, and every sign of a turn,
in domestic and foreign policy, and he
was the adored husband of the Queen of
England. " Through more than twenty
years, which flowed past like one long,
unclouded summer day "—the words are
Gladstone's—their lives were one.

No woman ever leaned more fondly, and no Queen
had ever had so much cause to lean. . . . Even among
happy marriages this marriage was exceptional, so
nearly did the union of thought, heart, and action
both fulfil the ideal, and bring duality near to the
borders of identity.

That in this combination of circumstances
the Prince Consort should have become
virtually joint-Sovereign was neither won-

218

derful nor, in spite of constitutional
grumblers, regrettable. The law of nature
gave in reality what an Act of Parliament
could only have given in form, and Prince
Albert was, for all practical purposes, a
King. Those who wish to understand the
mind and character of Queen Victoria must
consult the letters and journals which she
wrote before 1841 ; and (if their lives are
spared) those which she wrote after 1861.
In the intervening twenty years they may
indeed be reading the Queen's words, but
they are conversing with the Prince's
mind ; and in that mind they may perhaps discover reasons for the unquestionable fact that the Prince was unpopular.
Those who knew him intimately admired
and respected him; but the English people
generally, and not least the aristocracy,
misunderstood and disliked him. It is a
sorry confession ; but, when we remember
the social and ethical tradition of England
under George IV and William IV, it seems
obvious that the Prince's unpopularity was
due, in large part, to his virtues. In a

debauched and profligate age, he had set from early youth an example of manly rectitude. At a time when drunkenness was less a disgrace than an accomplishment, he was rigidly abstemious. Whereas the Princes of the former generation had spent their lives in accumulating debts which the nation had to pay, he sedulously kept his expenditure within the limits of his income. But not his virtues only —his very accomplishments—were charged against him as offences. To a generation which had only just left off cock-fighting, and which still patronized the Prize Ring, there was something offensive in the notion of a young man who played the piano, composed music, and etched.

In the displeasure of the younger " Bloods," who were the Prince's most persistent detractors, there may have even been a spice of jealousy. The Prince was brilliantly good-looking, though with a type of beauty neither English nor German ; and he had secured in marriage a hand to which others had aspired. The Queen herself has told us of a remark which, in the first year of her reign, she made to Lord Melbourne :—" I observed that marrying a subject was making yourself so much their equal, and brought you so in contact with the whole family." But it is not impossible that the Duke of Carabas and Lord Tomnoddy were blind to these disadvantages, and saw much to dislike in the successful wooer from over the seas. They avenged themselves in the oddest way. They ridiculed the Prince because he disliked long sittings over after-dinner wine ; and again because, after a morning's shooting, he went home for luncheon. They said he could not ride, and were dumbfounded with astonishment when they saw him going well with the Belvoir hounds. They accused him of cowardice, or at least sympathy with cowardice, because he set his face against the damn-able wickedness of duelling. Oddest of all, they affirmed that he was a Roman Catholic in disguise, whereas he was a Lutheran with latitudinarian sympathies.

221

Some more obvious reasons for unpopularity could be traced in the Prince's character and conduct. In the first place, he was undeniably a foreigner, and seventy years ago foreigners were quite as unpopular in England as they are to-day. Of course the Royal Family were of German extraction; but from long residence in the country had lost nearly all trace of Germanism. Queen Victoria's uncles had been bluff English gentlemen, of gracious presence and hearty bearing; properly dignified on public occasions, but overflowing with jollity in private life; and it was an abrupt change from them to this reserved and meditative stripling. Gladstone, who loved him sincerely, has recorded a trait which certainly could not conduce to popularity :—

A mildly foreign mark upon his exterior and manner, together with a perpetual endeavour to turn every man's conversation, every man's particular gift and knowledge, to account for his own mental improvement, most laudable as it was, yet may have prevented his attaining that charm of absolute ease in his intercourse with the world which he possessed in the circle of his family.

222

That thirst for information, though, as Gladstone calls it, " most laudable," must have been a little uncomfortable in society, especially when the person questioned did not feel very sure of his ground ; and the lack of " ease " in the Prince's public manner made an unfavourable impression on those who had no opportunity of seeing him in private life. He was thought to insist unduly on small points of etiquette, and to be horrified if a guest stood on the hearthrug after dinner. It was reported that the Queen said to a delicate lady : " Pray sit down, and, when the Prince comes into the room, Lady Douro " (an ample matron) " can stand in front of you." People saw the ladies of the Court standing in the Royal Opera Box while the Prince sate through the long performance. Thackeray, in the *Book of Snobs*, made fun of the ritual of Royal shooting, as depicted in the *Court Circular*. In a word, people thought the Prince too stiff.

The thirst for information which Glad-

stone described was allied in the Prince
with a love of instructing. Not only in
affairs of State and diplomacy, but in
almost every department of national life,
he caused his views to be made known.
In things military and naval, in matters
affecting Public Education, Public Health,
and the Dwellings of the Poor, in every
form of art, and in every development of
science, he was ready with theories and
advice. Perhaps the most remarkable instance of this all-pervading activity is the
letter which he addressed to Samuel Wilberforce on his elevation to the Episcopate.
The writer of the letter was then twenty-
six years old, a foreigner by birth and
education who had lived four years in
England, and a Lutheran by religious profession. The recipient of the letter was
forty, an Englishman by birth and education, reared in the strictest traditions of
English Churchmanship, and himself in turn
a Parish Priest, an Archdeacon, a Dean,
and now "a called Apostle." The letter
is a serene and thoughtful discourse on

the duties of an English Bishop; the line which he should take in Parliament, and the attitude which he ought to maintain towards those of "other confessions." It is certainly a remarkable composition; and it is only fair to add that it concludes with a half-tone of apology: " I have spoken as thoughts have struck me, and am sure you will be better able than I am to take a comprehensive view of the position."

Perhaps enough has now been said to account for the fact that the Prince Consort was unpopular, and more than enough to explain the violent reaction which ensued on his death. On the 23rd of April, 1862, Gladstone, speaking in Manchester before " the Association of Lancashire and Cheshire Mechanics' Institutes," said : " In the ancient Palace of our Kings a Woman's heart lies bleeding "; and the unanimous outburst of sympathy with the widowed Queen was accompanied by sincere though unavailing regrets. All at once the nation realized what the Queen had lost. The clouds of misapprehension and injustice were blown away by the breath of a new spirit, and people saw revealed a character singularly pure, lofty, and duty-loving, and a life devoted to the service of England. The reaction ran, as popular reactions commonly run, to ridiculous excess. The face of the country was studded with memorials to the Prince, like knots in network, and books purporting to describe his character and tell his life poured from the press. Besides a vast profusion of these un-authorized efforts, the Queen in 1867 commanded the publication of *The Early Years of the Prince Consort*. This was followed by *Leaves from the Journal of our Life in the Highlands*, written by the Queen herself. The Prince's Speeches were edited, with an instructive Introduction, by Sir Arthur Helps. Between the years 1875 and 1880 the Authorized Life of the Prince Consort was published in instalments by Sir Theodore Martin. Quite recently we have had three volumes of the Queen's Letters and two of her Early Journals,

226

in all of which Prince Albert plays a prominent part; not to mention the innumerable host of *Memoirs* and *Recollections* by various onlookers who from time to time came in contact with him. Lord Esher tells us, in solemn tones, that " it may be many years before it would be wise or prudent to make public any more of the private history of Queen Victoria's reign." So far as that history concerns the Prince Consort, we have already had enough of it. Abundant material is now available for any one who wishes to estimate the character of that remarkable man, and to place him in due relation with the events of his time. A persistent attempt to exaggerate his greatness, and to insist on all his opinions as infallibly true, can only result in the production of unpleasant counterblasts, such as *The Married Life of Queen Victoria*. In that book much labour has been misapplied to the collection of every scurrilous rhyme and paragraph, and every insolent caricature, by which malicious partisans

229

chose to annoy the Prince, and through him the Queen; his smallest foibles and errors are held up to contumely, some of his most conspicuous virtues are ridiculed or denied, and his married life is represented as a series of mortifications. Yet even the writer of that ill-conditioned book was forced to end upon the note of eulogy :— " The lasting work of the Prince Consort was not that upon which he had expended his energies and his life, for he did not increase the Monarchical power in England —it was the pulling of the Crown permanently out of the Georgian mud, and proving that those in high places could be virtuous and intellectual."

III

MISS JENKINS AND THE DUKE

" SURE enough ! it is Rip Van .Winkle—
it is himself ! Welcome home again, old
neighbour ! Why, where have you been
these twenty long years ? "

" Rip's story was soon told, for the whole
twenty years had been to him but as
one night. The neighbours stared when
they heard it ; some were seen to wink
at each other, and put their tongues in
their cheeks."

Washington Irving must, I suppose, be
included in that remarkable company of
authors (containing Scott, Macaulay, Dickens,
and George Eliot) of whom the High-
brows tell us that " nobody reads them
now." But I belong to a less supercilious
generation, and *The Sketch Book,* with
Irving's delightful version of Rip Van

Winkle's history, recurred to my memory
when I read, in the 'Cornhill 'Magazine, a
paper by Dr. W. H. Fitchett on "A
Curious Chapter in Wellington's Life."

Dr. Fitchett's slumber seems to have
lasted even longer than Van Winkle's, for
the world has been acquainted with
" Miss J.," and her remarkable flirtation,
ever since the year 1889. In that year
an American firm published *The Letters
of the Duke of Wellington to 'Miss f.,*
1834-1851," and they were promptly reproduced in England by the enterprise of
Mr. T. Fisher Unwin. I do not know
whether the book attained any wide circu-
lation, but among such as are interested
in the curiosities of literature it was
welcomed with effusion. It became, like
*Leaves from the Journal of our Life in
the Highlands,* and *The Diary of a Nobody,*
the oracle of a circle. It was freely
quoted, and copiously reviewed. Some of
its choicest phrases became catchwords. An
enormous discourse founded on it, as a
sermon is founded on a text, may be read

230

in the *Spectator* for the 11th of January,
1890, and no one who remembers the spirit
of that exemplary paper, when Hutton ruled
it, will be surprised to learn from it that
the Duke of Wellington, " deep down in
his nature was religious—a firm, reverent
believer." It was inevitable that a critic
who took this view should misunderstand
the correspondence, which reveals nothing
of the Duke's beliefs, but a great deal
of Miss J.'s.

While serious people took the book
seriously,

Historians add that there were some who laughed.

They believed that the whole affair was
an ingenious hoax, designed to attract
dollars by the spell of aristocratic mystery ;
and there certainly was a good deal to
justify this unworthy suspicion. The book
purported to be edited by " Christine Terhune Herrick "—a name which in itself
conveys a sense of unreality—and to be
compiled from a mass of papers which
had " lain for years in a trunk in the attic

of a country house within thirty miles of New York City." It does not need a very sceptical temper to suspect fraud in a literary curiosity thus engendered.

While some were thus swayed by external evidence, others found internal evidence not less damaging. If I remember aright, the late Duke of Wellington pronounced unhesitatingly against the genuineness of the letters, founding himself on the fact that they constantly refer to " Strathfieldsaye," whereas his grandfather always contracted the word into " S.-Saye," or, if he wrote it in full, spelled it " Stratfieldsaye." One theory was that the discoverer or inventor of the letters had created a " Miss J." out of some confused recollections of a lady celebrated in her day—" Mrs. Jones of Pantglas " —whom the Duke was known to hold in high esteem.[1] Another possible candidate

---

[1] This lady, born Margaret Charlotte Campbell, was a niece of Lord Chancellor Campbell, and became by her second marriage Lady Levinge. The letters which she received from the Duke of Wellington were published a few years ago in an American review.

for the honour of being " Miss J." was
the Hon. Mary Ann Jervis, whom the Duke
always called " The Syren." [1]   Although,
on his own showing, he was " old enough
to be her great-grandfather," he paid her
elaborate attentions, and corresponded with
her freely.   Miss Jervis, on the other hand,
made no secret of her willingness to be
Duchess of Wellington.

So the laughers laughed, and the critics
criticized ; but the present writer, although
he was fully alive both to the positive
comicality, and to the possible humbug,
of the whole affair, always held fast to
the belief that the letters were genuine.
He—or to speak more simply, I—had been
trained, by those who remembered the Duke,
to remark the strong common-sense which
always characterized his utterances ; and
common-sense is precisely the quality which
is most conspicuous in these letters.   Furthermore, I was a student of style and I

[1] This lady was a daughter of the second Lord
St. Vincent, and was married first to David Dyce
Sombre and secondly to Lord Forester.

did not believe that there was a writer alive who could imitate so exactly the Duke's epistolary mannerisms. After a lapse of ten years, my faith was rewarded by proof. In 1899 Sir Herbert Maxwell published his excellent *Life of Wellington,* and in it he dealt at length with the case of " Miss J.," writing neither as a convinced believer nor as a formal sceptic. After the book had been printed, but before it was published, Sir Herbert discovered that the Duke's letters " were in the hands of a private collector," [1] who permitted him to examine them. " Having done so critically, I have not the slightest hesitation in pronouncing them to be genuine. There remains not a shadow of doubt that all the letters are in the Duke's own hand. Most of them are addressed to Miss A. M. Jenkins, No. 42 Charlotte Street, Portland Place, a few having been sent to the care of a tradesman in the same street. The discrepancy in the spelling of Strathfield-

[1] *Qy*—Lord Rosebery ?

saye arises from the printer of the letters having extended the Duke's contraction, S-Saye, into the full name."

Since 1899 we have all had a good deal to think about, and attention has been diverted from the Duke of Wellington's flirtations to topics of more pressing interest. Dr. Fitchett, living apparently in a happy remoteness from actual affairs, has done a good service to the public by recalling its attention to a really amusing and forgotten book. But his interpretation of the correspondence does not convince me, and I shall restate the case as it presents itself to a mundane mind

Anna Maria Jenkins (1814-62) belonged, we are told, to "the smaller English gentry," and was an orphan. She was profoundly, practically, and enthusiastically religious; and, using the word "enthusiastic" in the sense in which it was used in the eighteenth century, I mean no disparagement. Her religion was of the Evangelical type, and she evangelized wherever she went, even minister-

ing to a murderer in the condemned cell,
and leading him to confession and repent-
ance. " It was not so common then as
now to make pets of condemned prisoners ;
and the success of this young girl in
subduing a man with whom priests and
parsons had hopelessly laboured, created
a sensation and called forth comment from
the Press."

By a transition of ideas not easily
traceable, Miss Jenkins came to think that,
after shriving the murderer, her next duty
was to convert the Duke of Wellington,
who was now sixty-five years old, conqueror of Napoleon, ex-Prime Minister of
England, and—what is perhaps more to
her purpose—a widower. It is only fair
to Miss Jenkins to say that she never
concealed from herself the fact that she
wished to be Duchess of Wellington.
" She believed it was the will of God
that she should become the wife of the
Duke." But, as she had in girlhood refused
a suitor because he was not sufficiently
religious, so now she determined to con-

236

vert the Duke before she became his wife.
With this high end in view, she addressed
to him, on the 15th of January, 1834, a letter
"on the necessity of a *new birth* unto
righteousness"; and three days later the
Duke wrote his answer—the first of the
390 letters which compose the series.
Curiously enough, this letter was not pre-
served; but we are told that the Duke
made two blots and put a wrong date,
and these symptoms Miss Jenkins attri-
buted to "the feelings which overwhelmed
him on the receipt of my epistle." Three
months later Miss Jenkins, who had now
come to live in London, went to Apsley
House, and left there for the Duke's
acceptance a Bible, with "a suitable note."
To this note the Duke replied that he
would like to meet the writer; Miss Jenkins
immediately conceded the privilege, and
asked the Duke to call on her. The great
man replied: "Although the Duke is not
in the habit of visiting young unmarried
ladies with whom he is not acquainted,
he will not decline to attend Miss J."

And on the 12th of November, 1834, the first interview took place.

Here it is necessary to mention one all-important trait which was omitted above. We are told that Miss Jenkins was "a very beautiful woman." In all ages of the Church, beautiful saints have exercised great power over inflammable sinners; and the Duke, who had seen much of beauty but not much of saintship, seems to have succumbed instantly to the double spell. When the day for the Duke's visit arrived, Miss Jenkins prayed for divine guidance in every incident of it, "even my dress"; and she regarded it as an answer to prayer that, when her illustrious visitor was announced, she was wearing her "old *turned* dark merino gown, *daily* worn," and was not "decorated in any way likely to attract notice."

But, in spite of these providential precautions, the spell did its work. Miss Jenkins "offered her hand" to her visitor, who "received it graciously and respectfully." The oddly assorted couple then sat

down, one on each side of the fire-place ;
Miss Jenkins produced her " *large*, beautiful
Bible," opened it at the third chapter of
St. John, and began to preach on the
necessity of the New Birth, "pointing her
finger emphatically, with the solemnity so
important an occasion demanded." The
sermon was abruptly closed, for the Duke,
from whom "all power of speech seemed
to be withdrawn," suddenly seized the
preacher's hand and exclaimed : " Oh ! *how*
I *love* you ! *how* I *love* you ! " This was
his first utterance—and quite enough, too,
for a first visit.

When the Duke took his leave, he asked
Miss Jenkins to write to him, and this
she promised to do ; but she felt what
Quakers call " a stop in her mind," and
did not keep her promise. Twice the
Duke enquired the reason for this silence,
and, receiving no answer, called again. On
this occasion he behaved even more ecsta-
tically than before, exclaiming : " This must
be for life ! " But what was to " be
for life "? He did not propose marriage.

A fortnight elapsed, and Miss Jenkins, having considered the situation, wrote to the Duke that his visits had better cease, " as they are of so different a nature from those I anticipated." The Duke replied that he " entirely concurred " in this decision. By so replying, he irritated the lady past endurance ; and she wrote him a letter which faintly uttered the feelings of her indignant soul. She told him that, if she had suspected him of anything but an honourable intention, she would have " spurned him from her as a serpent whose sting was capable of producing not only instantaneous but eternal death "—with much more to the same effect. The Duke apologized ; friendly intercourse was renewed, and the correspondence waxed brisker than before. Very often the correspondents nearly quarrelled. The lady was beyond measure peevish, exacting, and ready to take offence. The Duke was uniformly good-tempered, though terse. Thus, if her overweight letters were returned, Miss Jenkins thought an insult was intended, but the

Duke quietly explained the law of franks
and postage. If the Duke sealed with a
plain seal, instead of his armorial bearings, Miss Jenkins thought herself treated
with disrespect, and the Duke explained
that the armorial seal sometimes got too
hot for use : if he used black wax, Miss
Jenkins must know the reason why. The
Duke wrote rather illegibly ; Miss Jenkins
misconstrued his words, and the Duke
wrote patient explanations. Once Miss
Jenkins was annoyed by a fellow-traveller
in a stage-coach who indulged in blas-
phemy. When this occurrence was reported
to the Duke, he took no notice, and was
sharply rebuked for his indifference to her
outraged feelings ; but he was quite equal
to the occasion—" I don't consider with
you that it is necessary to enter into a
disputation with every, wandering blasphemer.
Much must depend upon the circumstances."
Sometimes he substituted his initial for
his signature, and was promptly asked if
he intended a disrespectful familiarity : to
which he replied that " the most important

parts of a letter were its contents," and that he "never much considered the signature, provided he knew the hand-writing."

After this last instance of unreason on his friend's part, the Duke's equanimity seems to have given away, and he marked his annoyance by writing in the third person. Even worse — he burned her letters, and thereby, in her judgment, committed "a sin in the sight of God, in destroying epistles intended for his everlasting good." But, as she kept copies, no harm was done. Presently, the first person was resumed, and Miss Jenkins noted the change with unconcealed satisfaction ; she still kept a watchful eye on the Duke's doings, and never failed to read him a spiritual lesson when she got the chance. The Duke had a fall and bruised his knee, and Miss Jenkins promptly reminded him that "it is not in man that walketh to direct his steps—a divine lesson which I was so anxious from time to time to impress upon his mind." When the Duke got about again, he hastened to visit Miss Jenkins, and, when she asked him how his knee was getting on, " he appeared delighted, pushing up his chair nearer to me, which of course met with the withdrawal on my part *due* to Christianity."

During the year 1836 Miss Jenkins received fifty-six letters from her illustrious admirer. On the 15th of November, he wrote that he was coming to London, and was at her service if she wished for a visit. On this the lady comments as follows in her diary : " How little did the poor Duke think when he wrote thus that the great Lord of lords had decreed he should not behold me again for nearly, eight years—namely, until the summer of 1844. O how mysterious are His unerring ways ! " But, although the Duke did not see this enchantress for " nearly eight years," bodily separation had no effect on the exchange of thoughts. They corresponded incessantly ; she preaching, scolding, and complaining ; he accepting her rebukes, explaining, and when needful,

243

apologizing—" The Duke of Wellington presents His Compliments to Miss Jenkins. She is quite mistaken. He has no Lock of Hair of Her's. He never had one, The Duke is not aware that he has been guilty of *presumption*, of *daring presumption*."

As the Duke was born in 1769, it must have been about the year 1839 that he wrote the following rebuff. " What would be said if I, a man of seventy years of age, nearly, was to take in marriage a lady young enough to be my grand-daughter? " Poor Miss Jenkins! It was the rebuke of a vaulting ambition, which is thus expressed in her diary : " I looked forward to becoming as 'a city set on a hill, which cannot be hid,' conceiving such exaltation would admit of showing forth *His* praises *openly* before men." A subtle attempt in the same direction is reflected in a letter of the Duke written in 1840— " The Duke is very sensible of Miss Jenkins's offer of service in case the Duke should be sick or afflicted. The

Duke is much obliged to her. He is quite well. He has no reason to believe that he will have occasion to trouble her upon any subject whatever."

Influenced, I suppose, by motives of self-preservation, the Duke now ceased to write. From 1840 to 1844 Miss Jenkins received no letter from him; but, nothing daunted, she continued to ply him with advice, " as the Lord condescendingly influenced me." On the 10th of June, 1844, the Duke replied comprehensively to all these hortations, and professed himself " very sensible of your kindness in giving me so continually such good Counsel." The correspondence now resumed all its former briskness, and before long the spell of the enchantress prevailed. At the end of August the Duke again paid her a visit, being dogged, to his great annoyance, by a band of observers, who probably thought they had caught the great man in some discreditable adventure. This tiresome incident seems to have had its effect upon the Duke, for soon afterwards his visits ceased for ever. He was one of the busiest men in England. "I am employed," he wrote, "every day from six in the morning till twelve at night "—but, unless he promptly answered every scrap of written nonsense and paid frequent calls, Miss Jenkins gave him no peace. In June 1845 she wrote him one of her customary rebukes, "little imagining that the Lord of lords had decreed he should never call again, knowing far better what is good for us than we do for ourselves." In spite of this, the correspondence continued for some time on its accustomed lines; but a fatal rupture was at hand. Miss Jenkins took a cottage in the country, and required some money to furnish it. She consulted the Duke on the subject and he, apparently, by mistake, understood that she wished to borrow the money from him, and seemed quite ready to lend it. This suggestion she regarded as an insult, and rebuked in her most vigorous terms. But shortly afterwards she fell into bad health; her illness required a good many comforts, and her means were suddenly diminished to vanishing-point. In this step she boldly told the Duke of her needs :—

It would appear that it is the will of God to place my life, humanly speaking, in your hands, as the friend, next to Himself, most dear to the heart of
Yours devotedly,
A. J.

The Duke replied with prompt and practical kindness, asking what was the sum required, and where it should be paid. But poor Miss Jenkins, irritated by illness and poverty, treated these very natural enquiries as fresh insults. She had no banker, knew nothing of business, could not and would not answer the Duke's questions. She apparently thought it his duty to undertake the cost of her maintenance, without entering into details of more or less, when or how ; and, when he demurred to this erratic way of doing business, she told him roundly that she would " rather beg her bread from door

247

to door than receive a favour at such hands."

Iræ amantium—soon the correspondence was renewed : by Miss Jenkins with " changed feelings " ; by the Duke with unchanged patience. The lady still toiled indefatigably for his " regeneration," and he persisted in replying that he did his duty to the best of his ability, and could not concur in Miss Jenkins's view of it. On the 10th of March, 1851, he wrote the last letter in this extraordinary correspondence. It concludes with these words :—

I know well that Miss Jenkins's Mind is occupied by Reflections on Spiritual things ; and that she must despise the occupation of one who considers it His duty to serve the Public to the best of His Ability ! With due respect for Her Higher occupations, I hope she will excuse my adhering to my own Course of duty !

> Ever Miss Jenkins's most faithfully obedient,
> Humble Servant,
> WELLINGTON.

In September 1852 the Duke died. Soon afterwards Miss Jenkins left England to join her married sister in the United States ;

but "her peculiarities had developed so unpleasantly that the two could not live peacefully in the same house." She died in 1862, and was disinterred, twenty-seven years later, by Christine Terhune Herrick.

IV

A NEST OF WHIGGERY

THOUGH my title may be rather reminiscent of Shakespeare's " nest of spicery," still nothing offensive is intended. A bird reared in the Nest of Whiggery could never befoul it or belittle it ; though perhaps he might perceive, with advancing years, that it had some laughable aspects. " The Sacred Circle of the Great-Grandmotherhood," though used as a gibe by Beresford-Hope, was the expression of a serious truth, and the *Early Correspondence of Lord John Russell,* given to the world by his son, Mr. Rollo Russell, illustrates that truth afresh.[1] The book is a Book of Russells. On every page a Russell writes to a Russell

[1] *Early Correspondence of Lord John Russell,* 1805–1840. Edited by his son, Rollo Russell.

—Amurath to Amurath—and a Russell makes reply. Each Russell adores the Russell to whom he or she is writing, and the principal topics of the Correspondence are the virtuous doings of the other Russells. When a letter is headed as from or to " Russell," without prefix or suffix, the person indicated is Lord John Russell—afterwards Earl Russell, and twice Prime Minister. The rest of the family are distinguished by Christian names ; but, as those names were frequently repeated in successive generations, it is not always easy to discern identities. Thus the letters refer to two Lord John Russells, two Lady John Russells, two Lord William Russells, Lady William Russell, Lady Rachel Russell, Gertrude Russell, and, as in private duty bound, to " William Lord Russell, the Martyr." The Martyr, indeed, was well out of the way, having lost his head in 1683 ; but at the period which the Letters cover—1805-40—there were four William Russells in being, and to distinguish between them is a task which has sometimes baffled even the editor. Then, besides the characters who were palpably and by designation Russells, there are a good many concealed Russells lurking in the book—two Dukes of Bedford, a Duchess of Bedford, a Lord Tavistock, a Lady Tavistock, a Duchess of Abercorn, a Lady Georgiana Romilly. Trace the " Circle," and it is found to contain Gowers, Howards, Vernons, Capels, Keppels, Cavendishes, and Ponsonbys, all of whom figure largely in these pages; stretch it a little, and it includes (by virtue of relationship to the Russells) Byngs, Thynnes, Bridgemans, Seymours, Clives, Gordons, Montagus, Listers, Abercrombys, and Elliots. Outside the " Circle " so far as blood was concerned, but closely allied to it by senti-ment and aim, were Foxes, Greys, Lambtons, Spencers, Fortescues, Ellices, Fitzmaurices, and Lambs—in short, all the famous names of Whiggery. Macaulay, though born out-side the " Circle," had found his way into it by political affinity; Stanley, afterwards the great Lord Derby, was born in it, but

252

worked his way out; and Brougham, also an alien by birth, was sometimes inside it and oftener not. Moore sang its praises to an Irish harp, Horner and Mackintosh supplied it with a philosophy, Rogers feasted it, and its Domestic Chaplain was Sydney Smith.

I have thus enumerated some of the company who contributed to the Correspondence now before us, and it is time to turn from the writers to the things written. The letters are, as a rule, easy, familiar, rather slipshod, and, when the writer wrote an exceptionally bad hand, not always intelligible. But they deal with a momentous period, and with such controversies at home and abroad as try the pith and marrow of political character. Throughout they breathe what was best in the spirit of Whiggery—vehement hatred of tyranny and oppression, firm regard for law and order, patient zeal for cautious progress, and a proud contempt for pressure, whether applied from above or from below. John, sixth Duke of Bedford (Lord

John Russell's father) was a Whig of the deepest dye. " The principles of Whiggism," he said, " have taken such deep root in my breast that nothing can shake them whilst Life and Reason remain within me." He had been Viceroy of Ireland in the Administration of " All the Talents," and had incurred some censure for what was thought the undue lenity of his administration. In 1817, looking back over ten years, he wrote : " I was urged to resort to strong measures and put in force the Insurrection Act. I felt convinced in my own mind that the ordinary operations of the law, administered in a combined spirit of temper and firmness, were sufficient to put an end to the disturbances, and the result justified my opinion." The Duke's Irish experience dictated his English policy at a moment when England was seething with discontent.

If strong and conceive measures should now be adopted by Parliament, if the Right of Petition should be unnecessarily infringed, if the power of the Crown should be strengthened for the sole purpose of abridging the People's liberties, then indeed will the breach be widened between the Government and the

254

People ; then will distrust and suspicion take the place of confidence and harmony, and I foresee nothing but misery and calamity as the inevitable results.

Here speaks the Whiggish hatred of Tyranny, but the Whiggish mistrust of extreme counsels is not far off—

If a few factious demagogues have been talking to ignorant assemblages of the lower classes about Annual Parliaments and Universal Suffrage, the nonsense is justly scouted by the great mass of the community, and surely we ought not on such insufficient grounds to be called upon to "draw an indictment against a whole nation."

Naturally, the letters trace in some detail the steps which preceded the Reform Act of 1832, and the part played by Lord John Russell, acting under Lord Grey and in concert with Althorp and Durham. It was the great achievement of his long life, and it was attained before he was forty. In 1826 the "Borough Reeve of Manchester" sent him a Resolution of Thanks, carried at a Public Meeting, for "the important service which, as a Member of the House of Commons, he has rendered

255

to the Town of Manchester in furtherance
of its just claim to be represented in
Parliament." In 1831, when the fight was
at its hottest, his brother wrote to him :—

> You have raised a noble spirit in the country, far
> beyond anything I could have imagined. I know no
> sight so grand as a People roused from their apathy,
> determined to assert their rights and freedom. A few
> months ago all was gloomy, dark, sad, and ominous ;
> now all is cheerful, gay, happy, and promising. It
> is like the burst of spring after a severe winter.

That it proved possible to carry the Bill
through the Lords, without creating the
peerages which the King had authorized,
caused Lord John unfeigned satisfaction.
" The Pitt party," he said, three years
later, " has been weakened and not
strengthened by making so many dull
country gentlemen duller Lords. And we
should lose in the same proportion. Two
or three now and then may be useful,
but I should regret any large creation."
" Dull country gentlemen "—here speaks the
Whig whose various schemes of political
and educational reform have been retarded
256

or defeated by the landed classes. " The landed gentry are very respectable, and I have always found them kind and humane ; but they are certainly the class in this country most ignorant, prejudiced, and narrow-minded of any. The unedu- cated Labourers beat them hollow in in- telligence." This was written in 1835, but fifty years were to elapse before that intelligence was allowed to apply itself to politics.

In spite of strong prepossessions, Lord John's was always a receptive mind. " I am," he said, " very warm in political ques- tions " ; but however " warm " he might be in pursuit of a political course, he never was ashamed to change his views as circumstances changed—" ' Bygones are bygones ' and ' Alors comme alors ' are two great maxims in politics." By 1836 he had come to see that the settled policy of the House of Lords was such as to demand strong action by the Whig Government, even though that action approached to what a year before he had deprecated.

R   257

He wrote as follows in a Memorandum for the Cabinet :—

It is evident that a majority of the House of Lords are combined, not to stop or alter a particular measure, but to stop or alter all measures which may not be agreeable to the most powerful, or, in other words, the most violent, among their own body. Both the Tories and the Radicals have the advantage of a definite course with respect to this state of things. The Tories praise the wisdom of the Lords, and wish to maintain their power undiminished. The Radicals complain of a mischievous obstacle to good government, and purpose an elective House of Lords. The Ministers stand in the position of confessing the evil and not consenting to the remedy. . . . It is possible, nay probable, that if the Tories could see a steady and gradual creation of Peers, to meet their obstinate resistance, they would be disposed to yield. Before the passing of the Reform Bill they were coerced by the dread of a large creation, and by that alone. It appears to me, therefore, that this opportunity should be taken for the creation of eight, ten, or twelve peers, and the Ministry be prepared to advise a similar measure whenever it is provoked.

The love of justice was as strongly marked in Russell as the love of freedom. He could make no terms with what he thought one-sided or oppressive. Melbourne strangely held that the fact that a man was " a trader " necessarily disqualified him for the magistracy, apparently on the ground that his private interests might clash with his official duties. Russell replied that, " if the principle was worth anything, country gentlemen ought not to judge about hares and pheasants." When the starving labourers of Dorset combined in an association which they did not know to be illegal, he urged that incendiaries in high places, such as the Duke of Cumberland and Lord Wynford, were " far more guilty than the labourers, but the law does not reach them, I fear." When a reform of the judicature became manifestly necessary, and was resisted on the ground of expense, he wrote : " I am not deterred by that argument, so long as the object is to give the suitor justice. If you cannot afford to do justice speedily and well, you may as well shut up the Exchequer and confess that you have no right to raise taxes for the protection of the subject, for Justice is the great and primary end of government."

Although, as these extracts show, the interest of the letters is mainly political, they contain here and there fragments of lighter stuff. It appears to have been Sheridan who said of Lord Lauderdale what was often repeated of a later statesman (also Scotch), "A joke of ——'s is no laughing matter." Fox's useful maxim for debate was "to say strong things, but not in strong language." Shelley justified the immoralities of *Laon and Cynthia* on the ground that, being "much confined within the circle of his own thoughts, he had formed to himself a very different measure of approbation or disapprobation for actions than that which is in use among mankind." Melbourne's opinion of Archbishop Whately is worth recalling—"It is impossible to be with him for ten minutes upon affairs without perceiving not only that he can do no business, but that no business can be done where he is." Brougham's rule for social discussion, if not tending to make things pleasant, was, as he said, "simple"—"I always *oppose* whatever I hear said. If

260

A abuses B, I defend B, and *vice versâ.*" An author sent a copy of his book to Lord John as " an offering to one whose name is indissolubly connected with the Historical Literature of this country, and who has begun by writing, and progressed by acting, History." Surely the author must have been the young Disraeli? No ; it was Bulwer-Lytton.

V

DEMAGOGUES

WHEN the aristocratic reformer in *Sybil*
absurdly told the Chartist's daughter that
the Aristocracy were the natural leaders
of the People, she replied, with excellent
sense : " The leaders of the People are
those whom the People trust." The
demagogue must have the faculty of
making great masses of people believe that
he is in earnest, that he sees quite clearly
the ends which he would secure, and that
he will not flinch from a fight when the
time for fighting comes. It was one of
Lincoln's best sayings that " You can fool
all the people some of the time, and some
of the people all the time, but you can't
fool all the people all the time." The
downfalls of demagogues—and history records
plenty of them—occur when people dis-

cover that they have been "fooled," and that the orator who promised to lead them to victory was false to the cause, or shrank from the inevitable conflict. I say "the orator," for oratory has in all ages been the chief instrument of the demagogue. Of course the spoken word reaches only, at the most, a few thousand hearers, whereas the Press has an incalculable range; but it is the personal contact with an audience— the magic of eye and voice and tone and gesture—that gives the demagogue his power.

The nineteenth century was peculiarly rich in demagogues; they sprang from all ranks; they had been trained by various processes; they preached quite diverse doctrines; but they all had the faculty of speaking to great masses of their countrymen in a way which carried conviction and excited passion. Each had his turn, his fame, his following. Of each, successively, it was said: "He is the greatest demagogue England has ever seen"; but for most of them the end was failure and collapse ; and few indeed are their memorials.

I put Daniel O'Connell in the forefront of my list because he combined in the highest perfection the physical, emotional, and histrionic powers which go to make the demagogue. His voice of music travelled fabulous distances ; he played at will on every emotion of the hearer's heart ; he could dissolve a huge audience in laughter or in tears, according to the necessities of his theme ; and he loved his country and his religion with an inspiring enthusiasm. He lives as " the Liberator," but his reign was over long before he died.

If we give the first place to an Irishman, the second belongs of right to a Scotsman. Henry Brougham's ungovernable eloquence, with its passionate resistance to every form of tyranny, and its wrath, and bitterness, and clamour, and evil-speaking against opponents, was a tradition which lasted into our own day. Yet he vanished from public observation when he ceased to be Lord Chancellor in 1834, and lived till 1868 in unhonoured obscurity. O'Connell and Brougham were demagogues by instinct, but lawyers by profession ; and their training at the Bar was supposed to have developed their natural powers of popular appeal. But two of the most effective demagogues of the nineteenth century were men who owed nothing to professional training. Lord Durham (1792-1840) and Sir Francis Burdett (1770-1844) were men who, in birth, education, and personal qualities, typified all that is meant by aristocracy. Their traditions were those of their order, and their habits those of country gentlemen, sportsmen, and men of fashion. Each had the birthright of a commanding eloquence, each detested tyranny, and each was ready to suffer for his faith. Burdett's imprisonment in the Tower was one of the events which shook the autocracy of Toryism, and Durham's administration of Canada laid the foundations of her settled government. But Burdett lived to desert the cause of which he had been a confessor, and Durham died at forty-eight, crushed by the ingratitude with which his own party had rewarded his work.

In the stirring times which preceded the Reform Act of 1832 there were no more effective demagogues than " Orator " Hunt, the hero of the " Manchester Massacre " of 1819, who broke the domination of the Stanleys at Preston, and then was himself broken by recalcitrant Whigs ; and Daniel Whittle Harvey, who, after swaying the London mob as no one since him has swayed it, subsided into the Commissionership of the Metropolitan Police, and suppressed the disorder which he had formerly fomented. Harvey died in 1863, and by that time two notable successors had appeared in the democratic politics of London. One was George Odger, " the inspired shoemaker," and the other Charles Bradlaugh. Henry Fawcett considered Odger the finest orator he had ever heard ; and I have seen Bradlaugh subdue the turbulence of an excited mob by merely raising his hand. Odger died, as he had

266

lived, neglected by those who should have been his friends, and the dismal doctrines which Bradlaugh taught are as dead as the Hutchinsonian system.

The latter part of the nineteenth century was enlivened by two of the most consummate demagogues whom England has ever produced—Lord Randolph Churchill and Mr. Joseph Chamberlain. Each had an almost preternatural insight into the desires, emotions, and prejudices of the people to whom he appealed; and it is to be observed that, though in their popular speeches they took diametrically opposite views of questions purely political, they both dug down far below the surface of mere politics, and addressed themselves to the root-instincts of human nature. Neither created political opinion, as Bright and Gladstone and Disraeli did; so neither could be called, in the highest sense, a political genius. But each knew exactly what his hearers wanted, and gave it with consummate skill.

When names so famous have been mentioned, Mr. Lloyd George cannot be offended if he finds himself included in the company. From the extraordinary success which has attended his public speaking I am inclined to draw a moral, which, to me at any rate, is exceedingly welcome. People had come to believe—and men in high political place acted on the belief—that the right form of public speaking was dry, hard, clear, unemotional, " faultily faultless, icily regular "—even " splendidly null." A Parliamentary critic said : " Demosthenes himself would nowadays be no match for a careless and jerking speaker who had ground down his facts in the mill of Select Committees." But Mr. Lloyd George has taught us that, now as of old, the strongest appeal to the common people is the appeal of the emotions. Here is an instance :—

The honour of Britain is not dead. Her might is not broken. Her destiny is not fulfilled. Her ideals are not shattered by her enemies. She is more than alive. She is more potent. She is greater than she ever was. Her dominions are wider, her influence is deeper, her purpose is more exalted than ever. Why should her children not sing?

268

DEMAGOGUES

A statesmanlike discourse, committed to
manuscript or memory, reads very well
in next morning's *Times*, but the true
spring of oratory is the old Holy Well
of Romance.

IV

FROM ROME TO LONDON

" AT last he came ; the great man in a great position, summoned from Rome to govern England." In this sentence Lord Beaconsfield was describing Sir Robert Peel, who made that journey in November 1834. King William IV had just dismissed his Whig Ministers, and had commanded Peel to form an Administration. But Peel was travelling in Italy, and arrived in hot haste, " after a most extraordinarily rapid journey of twelve days only, travelling by night over precipice and snow, eight nights out of the twelve."

Mr. Asquith's journey has been performed in a less exhausting fashion, and he returns [1] not to begin, but to continue, the work of Premiership ; yet there are circumstances in his career which inevit-

[1] This was written in 1916.

ably suggest comparison with Peel, to whom of all his predecessors, he bears the closest resemblance. Both sprang from the hardy north and both from the commercial class. Both had covered themselves with glory at school and at Oxford. Both were endowed by Nature with an inexhaustible faculty for hard work. Both had exceptionally strong constitutions. In both the distinguishing quality was hard common sense, and both had very early contracted a habit of clear and accurate speech, as far as possible removed from eloquence, but admirably adapted to a business-like assemblage. Both were conspicuously free from sentiment and romance; both held strong but not fanatical opinions, and both were ready to modify those opinions and to change their course as the exigencies of public life seemed to require. In two words, both were consummate politicians. But there were considerable differences between the lots of the two men, and those differences made themselves felt both in their characters and in their actions.

Peel's father had accumulated great wealth, and could bequeath to his son not only opulence but an assured position; Mr. Asquith has pushed his way to the front with no other aids than the thews and sinews of a truly English brain. Peel, from his earliest days, had been trained by his father for the business of public life; when Mr. Asquith went up to Balliol he had, I believe, destined himself to the Nonconformist ministry. Peel was returned to Parliament for a pocket-borough when he was twenty-one; Mr. Asquith toiled strenuously at tuition, journalism, and law till he was thirty-three. Peel entered the Cabinet at 34; Mr. Asquith at 40. Peel became Prime Minister at 46; Mr. Asquith at 56; but Peel quitted office for ever when he was 58; and died at 62; Mr. Asquith at 63 is still Prime Minister and has, as we all hope, a long spell of vigorous life before him.

Just now, when for the second time a Prime Minister is "summoned from Rome to govern England," it is interest-

ing to look back, and to see Mr. Asquith
as his contemporaries saw him in the
'seventies :—

> I remember him, says one of these, at the lectern
> in Balliol Chapel, reading the lessons with a strong,
> equable voice, strange at his age, and with a curiously
> critical air. It was remarked that he always seemed
> to be arguing with the sacred writer, and to be
> conscious of getting the best of it. He had a lean
> and hungry look, with no promise of that broad
> solidity which now confronts the House of Commons.
> There was no eagerness in his manner ; he took
> everything with an air of confidence that often
> bordered on arrogance.

His academic career, as tested by
examinations, was sufficiently distinguished,
but his most decisive superiority was
attained at the Union. As an undergraduate he spoke very much as he speaks
to-day, in sentences so exactly constructed
that they might have been taken down
verbatim and printed without correction.
His period at Oxford coincided with a
marked decline of Liberalism. The Ministry
of All the Talents, which Gladstone had
constructed in 1868, was now, as Disraeli

S   273

said, " a range of exhausted volcanoes."
All its great work was done. The Irish
Church was disestablished ; the Irish Land
Act was law ; National Education was
made compulsory ; Purchase in the Army
was abolished. A series of blunders and
follies, cumulative in effect, was now beginning to destroy the popularity of Gladstone's
government, and every one talked, not without
reason, about a " Conservative Reaction."

In the Autumn Term of 1873, Mr. Asquith
moved a resolution at the Union to the
effect " That this House neither believes
in nor desires the Conservative Reaction " ;
but before four months were over
Gladstone and his colleagues had been
swept out of power, and the " Conservative Reaction " was a dismal reality.
In 1874 Asquith took his degree and
vanished from Oxford. The remorse-
less deep of professional life closed o'er
the head of Balliol's Lycidas, and people
who remembered him at Oxford used to
say : " What an extraordinary place the
Bar is ! There are Stryver and Buzfuz

274

and Snubbin, making their five thousand a year—and even young Pendennis and Percy Popjoy doing quite comfortably—but one never hears Asquith's name."

So stood the case at the end of 1885. Then came the Home Rule Kite, the sudden conversions, the defeated Bill, and the dissolution of 1886. Mr. J. Boyd Kinnear, an excellent Liberal, who, since the previous November, had sat for East Fife, declined to change his views about Ireland, and voted against the Home Rule Bill. The wire-pullers determined, if possible, to turn him out, and, having heard of a young man called Asquith, who spoke well and was willing to vote for Home Rule, they sought him, caught him, and sent him down to Fife—with what result we know.

Mr. Asquith's career since August 1886 belongs to our political history, and there is no need to recapitulate it here. Gladstone was four times Prime Minister, and his four Premierships together amounted to a little over twelve years. Mr. Asquith has been Prime Minister only once, but has already completed a term of eight years :—

Is there anything left for ambition ? When the highest station is gained, does the noble infirmity become a desire for incense and for smoking altars? Does the praise of men count for more in itself than when tangible prizes were still to be grasped? Or are there yet greater possibilities? To be leader of the dominant party in the State is no small matter ; but, if the Party system is in decay, there is room for a new departure. Can he create ?

This question was asked (not by me) on the day when Mr. Asquith became Prime Minister, and I leave it unanswered.

VII

THE POWER OF SPEECH

To every one who frequented the Oxford Union between 1870 and 1874 the name of Asquith was a household word. There were two Asquiths, brothers ; both, I think, of Balliol, and both distinguished undergraduates. But, when one mentioned " Asquith " in connexion with the Union one meant " H. H." The traditions of early oratory are generally misleading, but, in this particular case, tradition is amply reinforced by memory. In October 1870 —the first term of Jowett's Mastership— there came up from the City of London School a thin, pale, rather prim-looking young Scholar of Balliol, who immediately began to make his mark. He was said to be a Yorkshireman by birth, but a boyhood spent in London had obliterated all resemblance to John Browdie. It was understood th'at h'e had chosen the Non-conformist Ministry as his profession, and he seemed likely to play a part similar to that played, two or three years later, by Mr. R. F. Horton. He was an excellent scholar, though by no means of the Eton type; much stronger in his mastery of his books than in the elegancies of com-position. At Balliol a man had to be, whatever else he was, a reader; and, if he had any leisure left over from reading, and did not like boating, it was natural to bestow it on the Union. Asquith's leisure was more than most men's, because his method of reading was so rapid and exhaustive; and he bestowed it on the cultivation of his natural gift of speech. If the City of London School possessed an institution corresponding to " Pop " at Eton, or " Debater " at Harrow, I feel sure that young Asquith' led the House there, as he subsequently led a greater one. At Balliol he was heard with awe at the mysteriously-named' " Devorgilda," and

278

from his college his fame spread to the Union, which soon got an opportunity of judging for itself.

The verdict was at once, continuously, and finally favourable. Some young speakers begin on a high level, and gradually slip down. Some begin in very humble fashion, and gradually ascend. H. H. Asquith began on the topmost level, and remained there till the end. Not that he was what is called a "beautiful," or fascinating, or moving speaker. Pathos, imagination, humour—those Three Graces of oratory— were equally and conspicuously absent ; but he was cogent, even commanding, in argument, shrewd in detecting a fallacy, ruthless in exposing it, and ostentatiously contemptuous of what he regarded as superstition, ignorance, or delusion. " I can see and hear him now "—writes a contemporary— " without the smallest trace of boyish rhetoric or epigram, hammering out his theme in clear-cut periods of dispassionate argument." I believe, as I said on a previous page, that, even in those very

279

early days, his speeches might have been taken down in shorthand, and sent to the Press without the correction of a word. Five years is a vast space in the shifting life of a University; but for that period, and longer, Asquith remained the Plancus of the Oxford Union, and nascent politicians of a later day were told that the level of debate was no longer what it had been " when Asquith was President."

He took his degree in 1874, and very soon afterwards vanished from an assured position at Oxford into the treacherous waters of professional life, where the waves seemed to close over his head. But, even in that submerged period of his existence, he was not silent, though he appealed to other audiences. As a lecturer for University Extension, as an electioneerer for the Eighty Club, at legal Debating Societies, and (when the solicitors were obliging) at the Bar, he was constantly speaking, and always with the same verbal exactness and logical force. His power of speech was by no means his only equipment, for he was also a vigorous and incisive writer, in so much as one of his early eulogists thought it necessary to assure the solicitors that he had now abandoned the dangerous company of the *Economist* and the *Spectator*. But he was, as he always has been, a speaker first and foremost, and a speaker, not for the mere love of speaking, but with a definite purpose and a concrete result. In the earlier 'eighties one would have said that his speaking was essentially forensic, and that the Bar was the place where if he only got the chance, his triumphs would be won. It was his skilful cross-examination of the manager of the *Times* before the Parnell Commission which first won him general recognition, and even as late as 1895 Gladstone's verdict on him was : " Asquith makes a very good speech on a legal point." But in the field of politics even the hard-bitten hecklers of East Fife found him a tough customer ; and experience of the House of Commons, with regular participation in debate, con-

verted what had been a legal into a
Parliamentary style.

At first his speeches were even too
accurately prepared. " Faultily faultless,
icily regular," though certainly not " splendidly null." I remember an old Parlia-
mentarian saying : " Asquith would do
better if he took his chances a little more
freely, and risk the plunge without the
corks." But the habit of over-preparation,
though it clings to Second Reading speeches,
cures itself in Committee. When a man
has to defend or attack the niceties of
a complicated measure, against opposition
which may arise at any moment from the
most unexpected quarter, he learns to
trust to his stars, and his style gains in
flexibility what it loses in finish. Before
Mr. Asquith had been ten years in the
House, he could (with all due respect to
Gladstone's great authority) do much more
than make " a very good speech on a
legal point." He did not indeed quite
equal Sir Edward Grey in that special
quality of Parliamentary speaking which

282

consists in uttering an obvious truth in a convincing form; but for the ever-varying exigencies of official business in the House of Commons it would be very hard to beat him.

In one respect, and that certainly not the least important, Mr. Asquith sets an example to all public speakers—I mean his brevity. Of an eminent preacher who still enchains us, it has been said that he never used one word when twenty would do as well. Invert the sentence, and you describe Mr. Asquith's speaking. Alike the habit of his mind, his taste in diction, and the structure of his sentences, all tend to brevity. Few men, I should think, who have made so many speeches, have used so few words and have wasted so little time.

But, in spite of all its merits, Mr. Asquith's is not a style which lends itself to quotation. It is difficult to recall more than one or two phrases which had the power of sticking in the memory, or passed into the current speech of politics. In the

283

Parliament of 1892-5, when the House of
Lords destroyed or mutilated every Bill
which the Commons sent up to them, Mr.
Asquith truly said that the occupation of
Liberals was "ploughing the sand." In
more recent times, "Wait and see" became
proverbial; and "I draw my salary" was
re-echoed with enthusiastic applause. But
his latest utterance as Prime Minister was
perhaps his best: "I do not like the
title 'Dictator.'" For my own part, I like
neither the word nor the thing; and I
trust that my friend Mr. Lloyd George
will restrain any Dictatorial tendencies which
his colleagues may have acquired in Africa
or India.[1]

[1] Written at the moment when Mr. Lloyd George
brought Lord Milner and Lord Curzon into his War
Cabinet.

VIII

CONSCIENCE AND ACTION

IT is good for us all, now and then, to
be driven back from practice to principle.
It is well to consider whether our conduct, in any department of human life, is
governed by any moral law, or is merely
the product of carelessness or self-interest.
In reply to several correspondents, I have
recently been urging one particular principle—that Conscience, not expediency, or
convenience, should be our guide in political
perplexities. Few will be found to gainsay
this principle when stated abstractedly, but
now let us look at it "pragmatically,"
observing the effects which it produces
when practically applied. As soon as we
so regard it we see that it works quite
differently in different cases.

No two consciences are exactly alike.
Some are torpid, some lively, some seared

and horny through habitual misuse, some acutely and even painfully sensitive. Of the sensitive conscience in political perplexities a leading instance is supplied by Gladstone's retirement from office in 1845, when Peel proposed to increase the grant to Maynooth. Here was a young and successful statesman who resigned a place in the Cabinet sooner than be responsible for legislation inconsistent with his earlier opinion ; though now he was ready to support the very Bill which he would not be a party to introducing. No wonder that he was voted whimsical, fantastic, and impracticable—" a man whose conscience was so tender that he would never go straight." Charles Greville said : " Gladstone's explanation was ludicrous : he only succeeded in showing that his resignation was quite uncalled for." And Disraeli wrote : " He may have an *avenir*, but I doubt it."

The sovereignty of conscience never had a more eager champion than the author of the *Analogy* and the *Sermons on Human Nature*, and yet Butler prayed to be delivered from the " *offendiculum* of scrupulousness "—a real infirmity to which the highly sensitive conscience is naturally prone. If any man ever passed through a long life of public service without deviating by a hair's-breadth from the line marked out by conscience, that man was John Bright. He jeopardized his seat by opposing the Crimean War ; he sacrificed it by opposing the Chinese War. He retired from the Cabinet as a protest against the bombardment of Alexandria. He surrendered the friendships of a lifetime sooner than comply with the Irish demand for self-government. In each of those decisive actions we see the working of the principle that conscience is supreme ; but, when we come to examine the precise grounds of his decision against Home Rule, some of his admirers perceive " the *offendiculum* of scrupulousness." The world in general has forgotten the late Lord Carnarvon, yet for a good many years he filled a large place in the public eye, and seemed destined to fill a larger. He was

287

a chivalrous, patriotic, and accomplished gentleman, of great name and great estate —in short, an ideal leader for the Tory Party, if only he had not so closely resembled " that scrupulous good man " whom Cowper depicted under the name of " Dubius " :—

> He would not with a peremptory tone
> Assert the nose upon his face his own.

Twice he resigned office in the Tory Cabinet—first when Lord Derby conceded Household Suffrage, and secondly when Lord Beaconsfield was siding with Turkey against Russia. He returned to office as Lord-Lieutenant of Ireland, in eager sympathy with national demands, and found himself treacherously deserted by astuter politicians who had used him. Politically, his life was a failure ; morally, it was a triumph.

So far I have illustrated the working of my principle by the cases of men whose consciences were exceptionally, and even painfully, acute. I turn now, for another illustration of that working, to a man of a very different type. Nobody ever charged

288

the late Duke of Devonshire with the "*offendiculum* of scrupulousness." His mental nature was singularly clear, simple, and direct. His biography has made it abundantly plain that, throughout his long association with Gladstone, he never learned to understand his chief's mind, or to antici- pate his point of view. " The plain-minded Whig nobleman, educated at Cambridge University, honestly endeavoured to follow this great man through the bewildering phases of his strange career." When allowance is made for an anti-Gladstonian bias in the writer, this sentence is true enough, and the " honest endeavour " con- stantly landed the owner of the " plain mind " in political embarrassments. Again and again he felt uneasy ; doubted if he was right ; thought he ought to resign ; and, in short, experienced all the pangs of political indecision. The mere effort of making up his mind was distasteful to him, and that is an effort clearly required of a political leader who leaves his party. Twice he made the effort with notable

T   289

result. In 1886 he declined to join Gladstone in his attempt to amend the government of Ireland. " Mr. Gladstone and I
do not mean the same thing," he said,
and he was right. His second, and final,
severance with Party was 'forced' upon 'him
by his conscientious objection to Tariff
Reform. In opposing Home Rule, he had
deserted the Party with which his youth
and middle age had been associated ; in
opposing Tariff Reform, he cut himself off
from the Party of which for the last
eighteen years he had been the most
important member.

" Throughout his political career his
attitude was that of a man refusing to
be hurried," and his attitude exactly expressed his mind. His conscience repudiated
what Lord Goschen called " a gamble in
the food of the people," and forced him
to retire from a Government which played
with it. But in his case the operation
of conscience was quite unlike what it
was in Gladstone and Bright and Lord
Carnarvon. Those highly-strung natures

290

and rapidly-moving minds sprang to their
decisions. Their consciences were not
sensitive only, but impatient and im-
perious. The Duke of Devonshire moved,
not less obediently, to the law of conviction, but with an extreme and even per-
plexing deliberation. The mental exercises
which he underwent between the promul-
gation of the new fiscal policy in May 1903
and his resignation in the following October,
form a most interesting study in the work-
ings of the political conscience. That the
eventual result of those exercises irritated
Mr. Balfour into undignified ill-temper was
not surprising. Men who are mentally
alert are impatient of long deliberations,
and not least when those deliberations issue
in action hostile to themselves.

What, then, is the conclusion of the
whole matter? We grant that conscience
is the supreme guide in political perplexities, but, if our neighbour's decision
differs, however widely, from our own, we
are bound to remember that no two
consciences act exactly alike.

IV

MISCELLANEA

I

DESTINY

" SIR GAWAIN said, Methinketh this shall
betide ; but God may well fordo Destiny."
This Arthurian quotation supplies me with
the word I need, for I had found it difficult
to choose a heading for this chapter. If I
had called it, more amply, Predestination, I
should at once have run on the "rocky
dangers" of controversial theology. If I
had called it Determinism, I should have
frightened away every one except the Professors and the learned ladies. "Necessity"
introduces flippant associations, and the
memory of the Scottish judge, Lord
Cringletie, concerning whom a disappointed
rival at the Bar wrote :—

> Necessity and Cringletie
>   They balance to a tittle—
> Necessity knows' no law,
>   And Cringletie as little.

But the word "Destiny" covers wider ground. It represents a factor in human thought, which is by no means abstract, but has had a most practical and definite effect on human life. Ten thousand are the pleas which an uneasy conscience invents for shifting its responsibilities on to something else than the conscious and guilty self; and nothing is easier than to charge one's shortcomings or wrongdoings on Destiny. In ages less materialistic than our own, the conception of a spiritual destiny was made to justify the most ghastly crimes. Man was preordained to do certain acts; and, when he did them, he was merely obeying an irresistible decree, and was in no sense amenable to moral censure. Sir Walter Scott, one of whose most entrancing gifts was the power of weaving thought into narrative, made fine use of this sinister belief in the case of the intending murderer, whose purpose was defeated, and who himself was killed. As he lies stricken with his mortal wound, Dryfesdale murmurs in his agony—

DESTINY

Strange turns of fate ! I designed what I could not do, and he has done what he did not perchance design. Wondrous, that our will should ever oppose itself to the strong and uncontroulable tide of destiny —that we should strive against the stream when we might drift with the current.

And Douglas, as he bends over the dead body, says to him who actually dealt the fatal blow :—

I blame thee not, though I lament the chance. There is an overruling destiny above us, though not in the sense of that wretched man, who, beguiled by some foreign mystagogues, used the awful word as the ready apology for whatever he chose to do.

The " foreign mystagogues " might indeed, had they thought it worth while, have justified themselves by high, though perverted, authority. A little while ago I gave some offence by writing about the " Calvinistic travesty of Religion," which had upset a young man's faith. A critic wrote : " It is scarcely fair to charge upon Calvin, or upon his perhaps too zealous followers, the sole responsibility for the doctrine of Predestination. Unhappily he was a too diligent student of St. Augus-

297

tine, and, possibly, a too faithful Paulinist."
But, whether we lay the blame on Paul,
or Augustine, or Calvin, the belief in
Destiny was made to justify hideous
crimes ; and its effects in destroying mental
peace was scarcely less deplorable. I
suppose that it reached its consummation
of logical and ordered horror in the
theology of New England, and in the
spiritual influence exercised by such men
as Edwards and Hopkins and Brainerd.
The mother clasped her babe to her
bosom, and believed, with an awful shuddering, that, long before it had a separate
existence, its ultimate destiny had been
irrevocably fixed, and that, in the huge
majority of instances, that destiny was
doom :—

In no other time or place of Christendom have so
fearful issues been presented to the mind. Some
Church interposed its protecting shield ; the Christian-
born and baptized child was supposed in some wise
rescued from the curse of the Fall, and related to
the great redemption. Augustine silenced the dread
anxieties of trembling love by prayers offered for the
dead, in times when the Church above and on earth

presented itself to the eye of the mourners as a great assembly, with one accord lifting interceding hands for the parted soul. But the clear logic and intense individualism of New England deepened the problems of the Augustinian faith, while they swept away all those softening provisions so earnestly clasped to the throbbing heart of that great poet of theology.

It was the allusion to St. Augustine in my critic's letter that induced me to venture on this quotation from—what I generally detest—a theological novel. *The Minister's Wooing*, by Mrs. Beecher-Stowe, herself a New Englander, presents with rare force and fidelity the struggle between predestinarian theology and human love— and love carries the day, in spite of Calvin and all his gloomy crew.

When Calvinism was desolating hearts and homes in the New World, it was beginning to lose its hold on England. It was in 1770 that the Methodist Conference made its ever-memorable decision, and, in spite of the enormous force wielded by George Whitefield and his friends, declared for universal redemption. Calvinism drove Cowper mad, and so wrecked one of the

299

most beautiful of human spirits. Mindful
of what my critic said, I will not lay the
blame on this teacher or on that; but
against the theory that God has pre-
destined some of His creatures to eternal
misery I will set the Church's faith that
God has created all His creatures for
eternal happiness, but has left them a free
choice to accept or reject the boon. It
was a theologian [1] pre-eminent for Orthodoxy
who wrote—" Hell may be, after all, only the
last awful prerogative of the human will ",;
and it was a Cardinal who said to me—
" I believe in an eternal Hell, eternally
empty."

But all these considerations belong, more
or less closely, to the realm of theology,
and, as such, will by some readers be dismissed with proper contempt. Let me turn,
therefore, to another quarter, not at all
theological, where the doctrine of Destiny
has had disastrous effects. In this quarter
the fetish is called Heredity, and it is
made to bear all those moral reproaches

[1] J. R. Illingworth.

which aforetime were heaped on the head of Predestination; and Heredity is reinforced by a convenient ally called Environment. A perverted spiritualism produced reaction, and the reaction took a materialistic form. Charles Kingsley was one of the earliest of our religious teachers to give the body its due place, and the things of the body their real importance, in the formation of human character; but it was his nature to overstate every truth which he held. Thus he put the language of the reaction into the mouth of Sandy MacKaye :—

Say how ye saw the mouth o' Hell, and the twa pillars thereof at the entry—the pawnbroker's shop o' one side and the gin-palace at the other—twa monstrous deevils, eating up men, and women, and bairns, body and soul. Look at that boy gaun out o' the pawnshop, where he's been pledging the handkerchief he stole the morning, into the ginshop! Look at that girl that went in wi' a shawl on her back and cam' out wi'out ane! Drunkards frae the breast! harlots frae the cradle! damned before they're born! John Calvin had an inkling o' the truth there, I'm a'most driven to think, wi' his Reprobation deevils' doctrines!

Another prophet of the Reaction was Oliver Wendell Holmes, who, in his eager revolt against the Calvinism in which he had been reared, cast the blame for moral aberrations on Heredity—a pre-natal inoculation with the poison of the rattle-snake—a drop of Red Indian blood unwittingly introduced into the straitest sect of New England Puritanism. And so increasingly for fifty years the doctrine of Heredity strengthened its hold, until some of our teachers laid it down that sin was merely a disease, and that we may be exonerated from the guilt of the most abominable crimes if only we can prove that our great-grandmother drank, or that our grandfather, when he beat his father, was repeating what the victim had himself done sixty years before.

Of more recent years, science has come to the rescue of common sense and morality; and now we are taught the obvious truth that each of us has an infinite number of ancestors, and that, while they have bequeathed to us an equal number of contending influences, it is our business to

302

decide which of those influences is to pre-
vail. So conscience and will have once
again resumed their kingdom, and we have
learned what our Arthurian forerunners
meant when they said that "God may
well fordo Destiny."

THE SPIRITS IN PRISON

MY title is taken from one of the most
mysterious passages in the New Testament;
but I am not going to attempt a theological discourse nor to perplex my readers
with doubtful interpretations. I am thinking
of those who, like ourselves, are

Confined and pestered in this pin-fold here,

but, unlike us, find one of the five ways
of exit barred. The physical senses used
to be called " The Five Gateways of Knowledge," but it is not less true that they
are five ways of escape from the cares
which " confine " and " pester " us. The
subject is forced upon my thoughts by the
spectacle, most pathetic, most exalting,
which just now encounters us every day
in the parks, in the streets, and in the

304

hospitals—the spectacle of men who, for their country's cause, have sacrificed what may well seem even more precious than life itself.

Mankind has agreed to regard the sense of Taste as the humblest of the five gate-ways. Honest folks who really enjoy their food are ashamed to say so ; and, as people undervalue the blessing of taste, so naturally they do not compassionate its loss. Yet I think that Dean Stanley, who was born without taste or smell, would have been a happier and a healthier man if he had been encouraged to eat by the incentive of the palate, and not merely by the feeling of faintness if the meal was forgotten. Harriet Martineau was born without taste or hearing ; but once, for a rapturous moment, the sense of taste was vouchsafed to her when she was eating a mutton-chop, and she exclaimed, in transport : " This is heaven ! " What would she have said if she had been eating strawberries and cream?

I mention Taste, only because it is one

of the Five Gateways. The sense of
Smell is infinitely more poetic, for the
mere mention of it recalls "the rich and
balmy eve," breathing roses and cloves
and mignonette and heliotrope and syringa ;
and, even when these glories have departed,
it reminds us of the wholesome freshness
of new-turned earth and new-cut grass,
and the strange, penetrating aroma of the
autumn woods. "Golden vials full of
odours " have their place in the Apocalyptic
worship, and who is there that does not
know the power of a long-forgotten scent
to wake a sleeping memory? One opens
a cabinet, or takes the stopper out of a
smelling-bottle, or unfolds a packet of
letters long since put away, and forthwith
the magical whiff of musk or cedar or
sandalwood carries one back over an inter-
space of thirty years, and one touches
again the vanished hand that locked the
cabinet and docketed the letters. The
loss of smell would be a very real privation.

The sense of Feeling is, I suppose, the
sense which most people value least. When

306

THE SPIRITS IN PRISON

Walter Pater brought out his *Studies in the History of the Renaissance*, he had them printed on a curiously ribbed paper, because life ought to be a series of physically agreeable sensations, and it was a pity to lose the gratification of the finger-tips. But this, though strictly æsthetic, was rather namby-pamby, and, except for utilitarian purposes, most men would suffer little from the loss of feeling.

The sense of Sight is, I suppose, the sense which we generally regard as the most precious of all. " Blind Bartimæus " is the eternal type of darkened humanity striving for the light. We all have had repeated occasion to admire the noble patience and courage of the blind, and our sightless soldiers are exemplifying it anew. By their endurance they make their souls their own. Blind men and blind women, poor, friendless, and bereft, yet bear the burden of life with unflagging cheerfulness, and cherish an even proud independence. Let any one to whom this thought appeals visit St. Dunstan's or

the Royal College at Norwood, and see
the marvels of activity and intelligence and
physical courage which are there the commonplaces of daily experience. Music is
to the blind man the very gate of heaven,
and through it the imprisoned spirit escapes
into light and joy.

There is an irritating commonplace,
glibly uttered by those who excel in
finding reasons why other people should
be patient, and it runs thus : " Oh ! but
blind people are so cheerful. It is the
deaf who are so cross and disagreeable."
There is an element of truth in the saying,
and the reason of it is surely obvious.
The time when one is talking to a blind
friend is the time when he feels his afflic-
tion least. For the moment he is on
even terms with those around him, and he
rejoices in his opportunity. We do not
see him during the long hours of silence
and solitude, when he is alone with his
own thoughts in a darkness which can
be felt. I always remember the pathetic
tone in which Henry Fawcett—the bravest

of blind men—used to say " Good-bye " when one left him, though it might be only to cross the room.

On the other hand, the hour of conversation is the hour when the deaf man resents his deafness. Every open mouth in the room, every animated face, every token of eager or interesting talk, reminds him of his loss ; and the vocal clumsiness with which people generally address themselves to the deaf aggravates the vexation.

What music is to the blind, that, I hope, books are to the deaf. A man may forget his prison-walls when he is visited by Shakespeare and Wordsworth and Scott and Dickens, and the goodly company which they bring in their train.

It constantly falls to my lot to speak on behalf of some society or institution devoted to the assistance of the " Spirits in Prison," and I anticipate some such opportunities as the result of the war. It is a joyous task, and yet it has its difficulties. The " Spirits," like the rest of us, have their prejudices and their predilections. They dislike, most rightly, any attempt at buffoonery. They dislike not less the feeling that they are patronized or talked-down-to. They dislike being publicly pitied. It is best on such occasions to say nothing about the pathetic side of things, for that side speaks for itself in a gymnastic exhibition by the blind, or a cricket-match played by two dumb elevens. A word of friendliness, a word of encouragement, above all a word of fun, is what the imprisoned spirit needs ; and thrice happy is he who, whether by voice or pen, has the privilege of saying it. " The lessons of Hope," said Gladstone, " are, upon the whole, the lessons of wisdom ; and the labour of life is cheered by the song of life."

III

EDUCATION

"IT is tiresome to hear education discussed, tiresome to educate, and tiresome to be educated." In this emphatic cry of Lord Melbourne (reported by Queen Victoria) the secret thoughts of many hearts found utterance. As to the tiresomeness of hearing education discussed, we all are agreed. In *The Lighter Side of School Life*, Ian Hay, himself a schoolmaster, has described with admirable fidelity the instructive eloquence of the officiant on Speech Day, who informs a jaded audience that education, etymologically considered, signifies the process, not of putting in, but of drawing out. Perhaps Lord Melbourne, in " his green, unknowing youth," had suffered under some such infliction. Her Majesty's journal thus elaborates the theme :—

Lord M. made us laugh very much with his opinions about Schools and Public Education; the latter he don't like, and when I asked him if he did, he said. "I daren't say in these times I'm against it, but I *am* against it." He says it may do pretty well in Germany, but that the English would not submit to that thraldom ; he thinks it had much better be left to Voluntary Education, and that people of very great genius were educated by circumstances, and that "the education of circumstances" was the best ; what *is* taught in schools might be improved, he thinks.

These words were written in 1839, and it is worthy of note that Melbourne, a good Whig and a friend to civil liberty, already detected the tendency to over-government which has made Germany what she is ; and, though thirty years later England submitted to the "thraldom" of national and compulsory education, some of our present advisers are apparently anxious to throw it off, or at least to mitigate its rigours. The State has got to economize—let it begin, say these publicists, in the school. The pitifullest and meanest outcry which can be uttered is the outcry of the well-to-do classes against expenditure on the instruction of the poor. To put the issue in the vulgarest form, com-

312

pare what, as a nation, we spend on drink with what we spend on education, and you will have good reason to be ashamed of our national housekeeping. Close on eighty years ago Sydney Smith, preaching in St. Paul's Cathedral on the duty of public education, said: "When I see the village school, and the tattered scholars, and the aged master or mistress teaching the mechanical art of reading or writing, and thinking that they are teaching that alone, I feel that the aged instructor is protecting life, insuring property, fencing the altar, guarding the throne, giving space and liberty to all the fine powers of man, and lifting him up to his own place in the order of creation."

Those are not bad words for a dignitary of the Established Church in the year 1837, and Churchmen may take a reasonable pride in the fact that, in the matter of public education, as in so many other spheres of secular beneficence, the Church has preceded and led the State. In the darkest days of social exclusiveness the

313

Church was the nursing-mother of the poor scholar, and provided of her own free-will that career for talent which is now secured by law. Bishop Butler, preaching in 1745 on behalf of the Charity Schools of London and Westminster, anticipated, and rebutted by anticipation, the views of those who a hundred and seventy years later should selfishly oppose the demands of popular education. He speaks of the successive changes in the world, and shows how they make certain knowledge necessary which was not so formerly ; he urges the hardship of exclusion from such knowledge ; and he ridicules with characteristic satire the absurdity and selfishness of those who are " so extremely apprehensive of the danger that poor persons will make a perverse use of even the least advantage, whilst they do not appear at all apprehensive of the like danger for themselves or their own children, in respect of riches or power, how much soever ; though the danger of perverting these advantages is surely as great, and the perversion

itself of much greater and worse con-
sequence."

The same great man in the same great
sermon says, with equal insight : " Of education, information itself is really the least
part." Most certainly it is, and yet, the
conditions of life for poor boys and girls
being what they are, information is a very
necessary part. The struggle for existence,
the pressure of competition, the rivalry of
foreign nations, makes it imperatively necessary that, during the few years that these
children are in our hands, we should supply
them with such an outfit in the way of
hard knowledge and definite accomplishment as will save them from being crushed
to death in the struggle for self-support.

This much must be secured ; and, con-
currently with it, there must be the moral
education which is supplied by order,
discipline, and cleanliness ; the sense of
membership of a body ; the encouragement of honest pride in good work ; some
provision for the æsthetic sense ; some
attempt to make good the inevitable shortcomings of the perhaps squalid home.

If this be so, it means, of course, warm, healthy, and convenient school-rooms ; it means something at least in the way of artistic decoration ; it means the cultivation of music ; and, above all, it means a well-paid staff of teachers. No form of public meanness can be more suicidal than that of " sweating " the men and the women who are training the next generation of English citizens. Physical exercises, such as drill and swimming—the training of the body as well as the intellect—should form a part of any system of national education. And this leads me to a further point— Can all this work of body and mind be done on an empty stomach, or, at the best, a half-nourished frame?

One free meal a day in every elementary school is, as I conceive, positively due to ill-fed children whom we compel to learn ; and, if any one is found to grumble at the cost, let him ask a teacher of a County Council school to describe the scraps of food on which, even in the depth of winter, so many of the children

316

subsist ; let him compare them with the succession of meals which he deems essential for his own family—and then pray God to take away the heart of stone and give him a heart of flesh.

Information, then, as Bishop Butler said, is the least part of education. The greatest, I suppose, is the development of the child's natural power to its utmost extent and capacity ; and the duty of so developing it must, I think, be admitted by every one who ponders the Divine teaching about the buried talent, and the pound laid up in a napkin. Unless we enable and encourage every boy in England to bring whatever physical and mental gifts he has to the highest point of their possible perfection, we are shamefully and culpably squandering the treasure which God has given to England to be traded with and accounted for. And we have no one but ourselves to blame if, as a Nemesis on our neglect, we lose our present standing among the educated nations of the world.

IV

A DISREGARDED PROPHET

ONCE, in those happier days when men's minds were not wholly occupied with bloodshed, Lord Haldane was discoursing on Education. " I wish," he exclaimed, " we had Matthew Arnold again among us to be our prophet." Arnold preached, all his life long, the doctrine that a State is responsible for the proper education of its children ; and this doctrine fell upon deaf ears. His first point was that at the apex of the pyramid there must be a Minister of Education. " Merely for administrative convenience such a Minister is, indeed, indispensable. But it is even more important to have a centre in which to fix responsibility." In Arnold's time the Lord President of the Council was theoretically President of the Committee

318

of Council on Education; but the work—
so far as it was done at all—was done
by the Vice-President of the Committee;
so authority was dissociated from responsibility, with the most injurious results.
,When Arnold had retired from his inspec-
torship he said to a gathering of teachers :—

I know the Duke of Richmond told the House of
Lords that, as Lord President, he was Minister of
Education—(laughter)—but really the Duke's sense
of humour must have been slumbering when he told
the House of Lords that a man is not Minister of
Education by taking the name, but by doing the
functions. (Cheers.) To do the functions he must
put his mind to the subject of education, and, so
long as Lord Presidents are what they are, and
education is what it is, a Lord President will not be
a man who puts his mind to the subject of education.
A Vice-President is not, on the Lord President's own
showing, and cannot be, Minister for Education. He
cannot be made responsible for faults and neglects.
Now, what we want in a Minister of Education is this
—a centre where we can fix the responsibility.[1]

This great and responsible officer must,
in Arnold's view, be a Cabinet Minister,

[1] Arnold's aspiration has now (1917) been realized
by the appointment of Mr. H. A. L. Fisher to the
Presidency of the Board of Education.

and was to preside over the whole education of the country. The Universities,
the Public Schools, and the Elementary,
Schools were all to be subject to his
sway. The Minister was to be assisted by
a Council of Education, " comprising, without regard to politics, the persons most proper
to be heard on questions of public education." This Council was to be consultative,
and the Minister was to take its opinions
on all-important measures, but the responsibility for the decision was to be his
alone. All such anomalous institutions as
King's College were to be co-ordinated
to the existing Universities ; and the Universities were to establish " Faculties " in
great centres of population, supply professors and lecturers, and then examine
and confer degrees. Then the country
should be mapped out into eight or
ten districts, and each of those districts
should have a Provincial School-board,
which should " represent the State in the
country," keep the Minister informed of
local requirements, and act as the organ

320

of communication between him and the
schools in its jurisdiction. All schools,
from Eton downwards, were to be
subject to this provincial jurisdiction, with
the Minister as the final authority. The
whole face of the country is studded with
small grammar-schools or foundation-schools,
having endowments, greater or smaller, and
a permanent and corporate life. These
schools, enlarged and reformed, were, according to Arnold's scheme, to be the ordinary
training-places of the middle class. Where
they did not exist, similar schools were
to be created by the State and dubbed
" Royal " or " Public " Schools. Arnold
contended that ancient schools so revived
and modern schools so constituted, would
have a dignity and a status such as no
school of private venture could attain.

Even more important were Arnold's sug-
gestions about the elementary schools :—

The moment the working class of this country have
the question of compulsory education brought home
to them, their self-respect will make them demand,
like the working classes of the Continent, *Public*

Schools for their children, and not schools which the
clergyman or the squire or the mill-owner can call
my school.

That word which he italicized—*Public*—
is the key to Arnold's whole system.
From top to bottom the education of the
country was to be Public. The Universities were to be made " public " in the
sense that they were to be supervised and
regulated by the State. The Public Schools,
traditionally so called, were to be made
really public by being brought under the
Minister and the School-boards. The
lesser Foundation Schools were to be made
public by a redistribution of their revenues;
and the new schools, public by virtue of
their creation, were to be established
alongside of the older foundations.

This, in broad outline, was Arnold's
scheme; but he saw very clearly the
" capital difficulty " of carrying it into
effect :—

The Public School for the people must rest upon
the municipal organization of the country. . . . But
the country districts, with us, have at present only the
feudal and ecclesiastical organization of the Middle Ages.

322

A DISREGARDED PROPHET

Of recent years people have come to regard education as far more a matter of public concern, and far less a matter of private venture, than in Mid-Victorian days. We have gradually come to see that the State and the municipality, in their respective areas, have something to say on the matter.

Again, the institutions of local government have developed themselves on the lines desiderated by Arnold in 1868. The subordination of education to County, Councils was, in the eyes of many, a risky experiment; but it was exactly the experiment which he wished to see. The resuscitation of the Edwardian and Elizabethan grammar-schools all over the country has brought the notion of the Public School to the very door of the middle class; and the provision of intermediate schools by local authorities has shaken the strongholds of such as Mr. Creakle.

The Parliament of 1868-74—the first elected by a democratic suffrage—was intent on reform in every direction; and the cherished right of a father to starve his child's mind was strenuously challenged. At this juncture Arnold repeatedly reminded his countrymen, then unaccustomed to the working of compulsory education, that it would be intolerably, unjust and absurd if it were applied only to the children of the poor. He contended that the upper and middle classes were every whit as much in need of an obligatory system, if their children were to be properly educated, as the working classes for whom it was proposed to legislate :—

The principle is just as good for one class as another, and it is only by applying it impartially that you can save its application from being insolent and invidious.

This theme is elaborated, with exuberant wit and fancy, in *Friendship's Garland*— a delightful book which all who concern themselves with National Education would do well to ponder.

V

GHOSTS

A FRIEND sends me the subjoined cutting; thinks it " Christmassy "; and is sure that I have some Family Ghost-stories which would interest the International Club :—

It was the Christmas gathering of the International Club for Psychical Research. The members, who are well known in Society and the professions, gathered round the bright little tea-tables and the blazing fires in a room overlooking Piccadilly and told ghost stories—stories of extraordinary happenings, of weird hauntings, and of things strange and most unaccountable.

Alas! I have no contribution to make. I cannot claim a place at that symposium. I am ghost-proof, and was reared in a ghost-proof home. My forefathers helped to plunder the Church under Henry VIII, and had their share in the Sack of Rome. Under Edward VI they suppressed a rebellion in Devonshire. During Mary's agitating reign they contrived to keep their heads on their shoulders and their money in their pockets; and then, acting under Elizabeth's commission, they restored order in Ireland by methods strenuous even for that age. Generally speaking, they bore their part in all the turbulent proceedings, at home and abroad, which made English History in the sixteenth century. It can scarcely be doubted that a family which behaved so actively at a period when human life was little accounted of, must have, sooner or later, done something which deserved a Ghost. Certainly they made a good many people ghosts before their time; and yet, as far as I know, we have been wholly free from supernatural visitations. Perhaps three hundred years of ordinary citizenship have obliterated the traces of tumultuous wrongdoing; perhaps the fact that one of ourselves was forcibly disembodied has redressed the balance and wiped off the score. Anyhow, the fact remains that,

326

as far as I am personally concerned, I have neither Family Ghosts nor Family Superstitions.

My friends have plenty; and yet, perhaps because I myself am ghost-proof, I have only very dim and confused notions of other people's ghosts. Vaguely I seem to remember that in every country house of any pretensions, from Hampton Court downwards, mysterious footsteps are heard, and doors open of their own accord, and people walk up and down stairs with their heads under their arms. Sir Frank Burnand got exactly the right " atmosphere " when he described the Haunted Chamber at Bovor Castle. " Childers wants tact. He hopes I shall sleep comfortably, and laughingly trusts I won't see any ghosts. I reply, I'll tell him all about the ghosts in the morning. I remember (just as he says good-night) a story of this sort in Washington Irving, I think, where a man jested about telling them in the morning about a ghost, and *was* haunted. I think his hair turned white, and he saw

327

a picture roll its eyes, and the top of the bed came down. I forget exactly; but it's not the sort of thing to remember just as you are going to bed in the ' Haunted Chamber ' of a strange house."

" Bovor Castle "—or at least the house from which it is drawn with curious fidelity —is in the cheerful county of Kent; but, as we move northward, ghosts become more insistent, and, when once we cross the Border, we are in their peculiar dominion. I suppose that as long as people talk about the Weird and the Uncanny, they will tell, with variants, the tale of G—— Castle; and at least one person in each company will know exactly where the Secret Room is, and what it contains, and what became of the rash lady who hung towels out of all the windows she could find, so as to localize, negatively, *the room which hadn't a window*. And, when they have exhausted G—— Castle, they will turn to W——, and will affirm that they met " Green Jean " in the passage and were surprised not to

328

find her at dinner ; or to A——, where, on
Hallow E'en, the murdered Countess still
points reproachfully to her bleeding breast.

I once asked a lady who, in her earlier
life, had lived in the very heart of society,
and who returned to it after a long absence,
what was the change which struck her most
forcibly. She promptly replied : " The
growth of superstition. I hear my friends
seriously discussing ghosts. In my day
people who talked in that way would
have been put in Bedlam ; their relations
would have required no other proof that
they were mad." My own experience con-
firms this testimony. People who used
to tell ghost-stories told them either to
fill gaps when reasonable conversation failed,
or for the fun of making credulous hearers
stare and gasp. Bishop Wilberforce in-
vented a splendid story about a priest and
a sliding panel and a concealed confession ; and I believe that he habitually
used it as a foolometer, to test the
mental capacity of new acquaintances.

" Superstition and infidelity usually go

together. Professed atheists have trafficked
in augury, and men who will not believe
in God will believe in ghosts." But of
late years ghosts have gone out of fashion,
and Spooks (a word fashioned, I believe,
by Mr. Andrew Lang out of Greek materials) have taken their place. People stuffed
with luncheon and coffee and Kümmel and
cigarettes will sit in an admiring circle
round some absurd impostor, male or female,
who dilates on "that rap, which none
who have heard it can ever forget," and
narrates imbecile conversation with departed
friends whom one had credited with better
sense. Closely connected with "Spook-
ery," is Clairvoyance; Mrs. Endor throws
herself into a trance, announces what she
knows will be acceptable, pockets her
cheque, and sets off on her return journey
to America or Australia.

But Clairvoyance is a little old-fashioned.
Crystal-gazing is more modish, and as easy
as lying. You gather open-mouthed round
a glass ball, and the gifted gazer reports
that which he or she can see, but which

is invisible to the grosser eyes. There are no bounds to the fascinating range of a crystal-gazer's fancy, nor to the awe-struck credulity of his dupes. But crystal is not the only medium through which a purged eye can discern the mysterious future. Coffee-grounds, though less romantic, are very serviceable. Our hostess is an expert in this form of science, and, being a thoroughly amiable woman, she makes the coffee say pretty much what we would like to hear—"Dear Mr. Taper, this is delightful. You will be Prime Minister before you die. Hope on, hope ever, and trust your star." "Oh, Mr. Stylo, I have such good news for you. Your next book will be an immense success, and, after that, Messrs. Skin and Flint will be more liberal, and you will make quite a fortune." Closely akin to the science of coffee-grounds is that of Palmistry. A wretched gipsy who "tells fortunes" at a race-meeting is sent to prison; but when the Vicar of St. Berengaria's gets up a bazaar for a military hospital, a

331

bejewelled lady sits in a secret chamber
(for admission to which an extra half-
crown is charged), and, after scrutinizing
your line of life, tells you that you have
had influenza, and, projecting her soul into
futurity, says that the next time you have
it you will get pneumonia unless you are
very careful.

Of these absurdities one can afford to
speak lightly; but graver reprehension is
required for certain malpractices which
are grouped together under the name of
" Occultism." I have known a most pro-
mising boy whose health was destroyed
and his career ruined by a hypnotic experiment practised on him without his parents'
knowledge. I have known a hypnotic clergyman who cozened the women of his con-
gregation out of money, character, and, in
some cases, reason. Where Occultism is
pursued, veracity and self-respect disappear,
and all that is evil finds congenial
lodgment. Whoso is wise will ponder
these things, and will give occultists, male
and female, an uncommonly wide berth.

332

But, in pursuing, I seem to have travelled a long way from my starting-point. To it I now return, under the guidance of Charles Kingsley, who, when questioned about his Family Ghost—" Button-cap " yclept—wrote thus to his enquirer :—

Of Button-cap—I knew him well. He used to walk across the room in flopping slippers, and turn over the leaves of books to find the missing deed, whereof he had defrauded the orphan and the widow. Nobody ever saw him ; but, in spite of that, he wore a flowered dressing-gown, and a cap with a button on it. Sometimes he turned cross, and played Poltergeist, as the Germans say, rolling the barrels in the cellar with surprising noise, which was undignified. So he was always ashamed of himself, and put them all back in their places before morning. I believe he is gone now. . . .

Perhaps some one had been laying phosphoric paste about, and he ate thereof, and ran down to the pond, and drank till he burst. He was Rats.

The last word in this instructive passage has acquired a new sense since Kingsley wrote, and it is a sense which exactly suits the matter in hand. Whenever I listen to tales of the Occult, the exclamation which rises instinctively to my lips is—" RATS ! "

333

VI

WHY THURSDAY?

" A MEATLESS Thursday " has a curiously perverse sound. In a novel by a highly accomplished lady there is a moving dialogue between the heroine and the hero at a water-party—" ' Sit in the bows,' she said, pointing to the stern." Why? and the same question rises to my lips when I see the Bishop of London combining with journalists, doctors, and dissenting ministers to enjoin a " meatless Thursday." A meatless Friday is prescribed by the Church of which the Bishop is a chief pastor, and is doubtless observed in all episcopal palaces. It is also prescribed by the Church of Rome, and it was observed, until a time well within my own recollection, by the stricter followers of John Wesley.

334

WHY THURSDAY?

The Church of England anticipated, by about three hundred years, the salutary efforts of Dr. Saleeby and Mr. St. Loe Strachey. The Church enumerates as " days of fasting or abstinence " (which certainly excludes meat) all the Fridays in the year, unless Christmas Day falls on one of them; the 40 days of Lent, 16 vigils of Holy Days, 12 Ember Days, and 3 Rogation Days—altogether (making allowance for the possibility that some may overlap) at least 120 days out of the 365. It is true that very few, in our degenerate age, can face the 40 days of Lenten abstinence, but every one can manage a meatless Friday, and thereby can improve his health, save his money, and illustrate his churchmanship. But I am a zealous champion of the rights of conscience, and would not for the world impose the Church's rule on my fellow-citizens who are not Churchmen. My Non-conformist brother can enjoy a meatless Thursday; the atheist, the agnostic, and the nothingarian, can choose a Monday,

335

or a Tuesday, or a Wednesday; and my
Jewish friends would probably prefer
Saturday, thereby training themselves for
the far greater feat of endurance which
they practise between sunset and sunset
on the Day of Atonement.

To establish one meatless day in seven
would be, without reference to any theological predilections, a social reform of
great value. The war has taught us that
many things, Conscription among the
number, which we deemed impossible are
possible, and, we hope, salutary. If the
war also teaches us that we all eat too
much meat, and can be not only, as well
but much better without it, we shall all
be the gainers. " Ils mangent comme les
ogres ! " was the comment of a French
maid on the eating habits of an English
family,; and a glance at a common cookery-
book or bill of fare will justify her verdict. Harold Skimpole was wise before
his time when he contrasted his own
habits with those of his carnivorous
contemporaries :—

336

Some men want legs of beef and mutton for
breakfast ; I don't. Give me my .peach, my cup of
coffee, and my claret ; I am content. I don't want
them for themselves ; but they remind fne of the sun.
There's nothing solar about legs of beef and mutton ;
mere animal satisfaction.

Legs of beef and mutton for breakfast
must have been a gastronomical excess even
in the days when Mr. Skimpole flourished ;
but legs of beef and mutton for dinner,
following one another in hideous alterna-
tion all the year round, have maintained
their monotonous ascendency even to the
present day. The first man who had the
courage to challenge this national abuse
was Sir Henry Thompson (1820-1904),
whose long practice as a surgeon convinced
him that a large proportion of human disease
was directly traceable to excess of meat-
eating. Early in the 'eighties he published
his excellent treatise on *Food and Feeding*,
and showed at once a wholesomer, a
cheaper, and a more agreeable, system of
aliment than had previously obtained in
England. Though he was separated by
the distance of the poles from the eccle-

Y

siastical standpoint, he enjoined a diet which
would come near to making every day in
the year a *jour maigre*. He claimed for
fish and eggs and vegetables and cheese
their rightful place in domestic economy ;
and, when I add that he also prescribed
water-drinking, I secure for him the
respectful attention of another band of
dietetic reformers.

The reform which Thompson taught has
made its way slowly but surely. The
consumption of animal food in the ordinary
diet of the well-to-do has visibly declined,
but might be reduced much further with
the best results. Of course, all tides are
liable to refluences, and all reforms to
reaction ; and there was a lamentable
recrudescence of meat-eating when "The
Salisbury Cure" came into vogue. I have
no notion why it was called "Salisbury"
—certainly not with reference to the illustrious statesman so named. It consisted
of minced beef, as nearly as possible raw,
with jorums of hot water between meals.
The tendency of all fanaticism is to cause

338

a rebound; and the victims of this disgusting cure as soon as they recovered betook themselves, with all convenient speed, to "The Haig Cure." This cure was cheese. A mountain of Stilton or Cheddar crowned the festive board, and the chinks, external and internal, were filled up with nuts. It is true of man generally, and of the food-faddist in particular, that he never continueth long in one stay; and the lively oracles of Salisbury and Haig were soon superseded by those of Metchnikoff. Constitutions which had survived red beef and hot water, cheese and nuts, succumbed to sour milk, which, by its very loathsomeness, gradually recalled people to dietetic sanity; but not for long. Now the enthusiasts are all agog for the " Fruitarian Cure," which has, at least in the summer, an alluring sound. We have sometimes shuddered at the rigidity of the monastic establishment described in *The Ingoldsby Legends* :—

Where a full choir of monks and a full choir of nuns
Lived on nothing but cabbage and hot-cross buns.

But the rigidity of the " Fruitarian Cure "
is much more alarming. It sanctions the
cabbage, but forbids the buns. It teaches
that all cooking is a mistake, that the
disciple must live on raw vegetables, and
that even bread and tea, being cooked, are
poisonous. When these dismal truths are
once grasped, one feels sure that a revolt
will ensue and that common sense will
resume its reign.

In all reforms, religious, social, political,
economic, the extremist is the pioneer ; but
wisdom consists in following him only half,
or at the most three-quarters, of the way.
By all means let us go in for the one
meatless day, in seven, and, if we can make
it two, so much the better. In health and
in patriotism, as well as in things spiritual,
the Church is a trustworthy guide.

VII

IN HONOUR BOUND

Edged with red, white, and blue bands, Lord
Devonport's pledge card was issued yesterday to
householders for exhibition in their windows. On a
white background it bears the inscription, in red and
blue lettering: "In honour bound we adopt the
national scale of voluntary rations." Copies may be
had free on application to the Publicity Bureau,
Ministry of Food, Grosvenor House, W. 1.

I COPY the foregoing extract from a daily
paper, because I wish to know what is
implied by the first three words of the
pledge-card. No man can be " in honour
bound " except by his own engagement.
No one on earth—not the King, not the
Pope, not the Archbishop of Canterbury,
not the Prime Minister, not even Lord
Devonport—can put another person " on his
honour." I repudiate the " red, white, and
blue bands " of the Publicity Bureau, and

cast away its cords from me. I can pledge my own honour, but no one on earth can pledge it for me.

To maintain the opposite of this proposition would land society in preposterous difficulties. If one man had the power to put another "on his honour," life, property, and character would all be jeopardized. That pleasant rogue, Raffles, contemplating a burglary, could say to his bosom friend : " I mean to try my luck at No. 1, Stucco Gardens, to-night, but I put you on your honour not to tell the police." That eminent sporting and poisoning character, Dr. Palmer, of Rugeley, could have said to a confederate : " I put you on your honour not to mention it, but I mean to give our friend Cooke a dose which he won't recover from." Thackeray's " dear young literary friend, Tom Garbage," might say to another young lion of Fleet Street : " I'm going to write something libellous about Lady Lilywhite, of course anonymously ; but mind, you are on your honour not to give me away." The claim

342

of A. to put B. on his honour, if allowed by society, would make B. a partaker of all A.'s misdoings, and might force him, all against his will, to compound a felony. Of course, if Raffles or Palmer or Garbage said to his friend : " Will you promise not to divulge what I am going to tell you ? " and the friend was fool enough to say " Yes," his honour would be pledged ; but by his own act.

Putting aside the extreme though illustrative instance of crime, only think of the disastrous use which the " Unco' guid," the Faddists, and the Fanatics, would make of the power to put other people on their honour. Archbishop Temple or Sir Wilfrid Lawson might have put us on our honour to abstain from alcohol ; the Food Reformers might put us on our honour to eat nothing but water-cress and arrow-root ; the Anti-Tobacco League might put us on our honour to eschew cigarettes ; and the Dress Reformers on our honour to wear vegetarian boots.

But, it may be said : " In these cases

343

there would be no executive authority behind the Faddist who is meddling with your honour ; whereas Lord Devonport, if you disregard his decrees, can enforce them by cutting off the supplies." But this does not mend matters—it makes them worse, because it introduces the element of bullying. If Lord Devonport thinks that we ought to eat only a certain amount, by all means let him enforce that amount—if he can. If he thinks he cannot enforce it, let him say : " I appeal to your patriotism and good sense to economize in food as much as you can "—and every good citizen will at once respond. But if he says : " I put you on your honour only to eat as much as I allow," every one who values the few shreds of independence still left to us will reply : " Here you are travelling beyond your powers. My honour is my own affair. If I promise to abstain from food, then I am ' in honour bound ' ; but the fact that you have told me to abstain, and threaten compulsion if I disobey, neither binds my honour nor touches my conscience."

344

I remember an incident of my Harrow days which illustrates Lord Devonport's method. The master under whom I began had a laudable wish to make us learn some English poetry, in addition to the Virgil with which we were daily crammed, so he proposed a voluntary repetition of Milton, for which he promised high marks. But we were young and thoughtless, and *Paradise Lost* seemed no paradise—rather a purgatory. Whereupon the master said : " If you do not act on my suggestion about the Voluntary Repetition, I shall be obliged to make it compulsory." This method of contingent, or conditional, coercion, was ludicrous enough ; but the master did not enhance the absurdity by saying : " I put you on your honour to learn Raphael's speech by heart, and if you don't, I shall punish you." Young as we were, I think that some of us would have replied : " Wait till we've promised, sir, and then punish us if we break our word." I have made no promise to Lord Devonport, and therefore I cannot break it. I have not pledged

345

my honour to him, and he cannot pledge it for me. Not all the Red, White, and Blue Bands in the " Publicity Bureau "— not all the red tape and blue pencils in Grosvenor House—can make me " in honour bound " to do what I have not promised to do.

I heard the other day a curious demurrer to my doctrine that no man can bind another's honour—" When you consult a priest, or a doctor, or a banker, he is bound in honour not to divulge what you tell him." Most true ; but I do not bind him ; he binds himself. A man who enters the priesthood binds himself in honour, and by the Common Law of Christendom, to keep what he hears in Confession as secret as the grave ; and the same effective though unspoken pledge is given in substance by every man who becomes a doctor or a banker. In each case the man pledges his own honour by the very act of entering his profession.

I have made this protest against what I think a monstrous assumption, but in making it I am not actuated by any disrespect for Lord Devonport (whose public spirit I sincerely admire), or by any dissent from the system of diet which he is trying to establish. Quite apart from all considerations arising out of the war, he will be rendering a valuable service to the national health if he persuades Englishmen that what Harold Skimpole called " legs of sheep and oxen " are not the appointed food of man. Only, if he is going to cut off our meat, he must induce his colleague, Mr. Prothero, to give us some potatoes. If that eminent agriculturist says that there are none to be got, let him turn his attention to a certain district of Bedfordshire, over which, as agent to the Duke of Bedford, he has long exercised a benevolent despotism. It is almost a pity that he cannot stand again for that division. " Prothero and Potatoes " would be an exhilarating cry.

VIII

HATFIELD

HATFIELD HOUSE is indeed one of " The Stately Homes of England." It combines all the elements of grandeur—scale and position, architectural beauty, historical interest, and a very real influence over a considerable town and a large district of an important county. In the winter of 1835 this sacred ark of territorial ascendency was nearly destroyed by fire. One wing perished, the Dowager Lady Salisbury (affectionately called " Old Sarum ") being burnt to death in it. The rest was saved by the exertions of family, household, friends, and neighbours, among whom one of the most active was a young Mr. Talbot, a cousin of Lord Salisbury. When the fire was extinguished the thankful owner called young Talbot to him and said : " You have worked right well, and have helped to save a great disaster. I will show my gratitude in a practical way. If you will take Holy Orders I will make you Rector of Hatfield, which is worth £1,500 a year, with a capital house." The offer was accepted ; Mr. Talbot was ordained, and retained the rectory of Hatfield till he died, at a good old age, in 1888. He was succeeded by Lord William Cecil. Lord William now [1] becomes Bishop of Exeter, and the right of presenting to Hatfield lapses to the Prime Minister. Here, indeed, is an instructive object-lesson.

In the first place, we see the principle on which private patronage in the Established Church is administered. (Let me say in passing that Lord William Cecil was, apart from all considerations of consanguinity, an exemplary Parish Priest.) In the second, we see the anomalousness of the system on which episcopal appointments are made. Mr. Asquith, who nominated

November 1916.

Lord William to the See of Exeter, is, I believe, a Nonconformist unattached, though the Moravians had a share in his upbringing. For ten years it was his official duty to choose the men who, within the precincts of the Established Church, should be made Successors to the Apostles. That is anomalous enough; but even more quaint is the third phase of the transaction. The Rector of Hatfield becoming a bishop, the law decrees that his successor shall be appointed by the Crown, and the Crown, for this purpose, is now Mr. Lloyd George. " Dod " throws only a very defective light on the religious views of M.P.'s, but I think I have heard that the Baptists claim our new Prime Minister as their own. Here the object-lesson is complete. An undergraduate helps to extinguish a fire; he becomes the Rector of an important parish for fifty years. He goes the way of all flesh— even clerical flesh, which is proverbially enduring—and he is succeeded by the patron's son, a curate of twenty-five, who

350

holds the same benefice for twenty-eight years. A barrister-Premier, who is a Dissenter if he is anything, turns this Rector into a Bishop; and the fiery apostle of Welsh Disestablishment — the suddenly chosen head of a War Cabinet—must appoint a pastor for the flock which the Bishop resigns. Surely the force of anomaly could no farther go.

I have exhibited this object-lesson in some detail, because it illustrates a system which is as repugnant to some Churchmen as it is to all Nonconformists. I have for twenty years presided over an organization called " The Churchmen's Liberation League," and I welcome the opportunity of stating the object for which we stand, and the methods by which we hope—some day—to attain it.

We stand for the principle of " A Free Church in a Free State." We desire to liberate the Church of England from the control of the State, because we believe :—

1. That State control enfeebles, and tends to destroy, the spiritual life of the Church, by encouraging

her to lean on the support of, and accommodate her teaching to, the Secular power.

2. That the Church of England, as a religious society, has a right to self-government, free from the influence of Crown or Parliament, and subject only to the Divine law.

3. That in a country where there are many forms of religion, it is unjust and invidious that one should be maintained by the State in a position of privilege and pre-eminence.

4. That the maintenance of an Established Church is harmful to the spiritual life of the nation, because it tends to foster a false conscience, and to make people think that National Righteousness consists in the legal Establishment of the Church rather than in the personal religion of individual men and women.

5. That the subjection of the Church to the State is an invasion of the Sovereign Rights of the Lord Jesus Christ as King of the Universal Church and Master of His own House.

The Disestablishment of the Church would, in our judgment, involve the following changes :—

1. The Sovereign would cease to be "Supreme Governor of the Church."

2. The Bishops would no longer sit in the House of Lords, but the clergy would no longer be disqualified for sitting in the House of Commons.

352

3. The control of the doctrine, discipline, and worship of the Church would be withdrawn from Parliament.
4. The Judicial Committee of the Privy Council would no longer have authority in religious matters, and Ecclesiastical Courts would cease to possess coercive jurisdiction.
5. Private and official patronage in the Cure of Souls would be abolished.
6. The Bishops would be no longer nominated by the Crown, but elected by the Church.

So far, I have spoken of Disestablishment only. But it is not likely that the State (as represented by Parliament) would consent to Disestablishment unless it were accompanied by some measure of Disendowment. All vested interests, whether of clergy or laity, would be fully protected, and the Church might reasonably hope to retain the use of the cathedrals and parish churches and the modern endowments. In this matter, however, we could safely trust to the sense of justice which is inherent in the English people.

It has been well said that " independence from State-aid calls forth energy ; the withdrawal from compromising situations or

z 353

unmeaning alliance leads to the concentration of force and the creation of true union. A Church to live must have a clear conscience, and, if its position in the State is felt to compromise that conscience, then, however advantageous such a position may be, not only for temporal purposes (though these are not necessarily to be despised), but also for the advancement of religion and morality, there must be no hesitation. That Church must make up its mind to depart out of Egypt, and to go into the wilderness."

In the strong conviction that " the wilderness " is the only way to the Promised Land of Freedom, we solicit the co-operation of our fellow-Churchmen in the endeavour to which we are ourselves committed.

IX

BISHOPS AND ECONOMY

THE excellent Bishop of London seems
unduly oppressed by that £10,000 a year
of his. He is even painfully anxious to
rebut the charge of wealth. The other
day his protest went up from St. Botolph's
churchyard—" Referring to his salary of
£10,000 a year, he said that the State
took half of this in rates and taxes, and
he had to keep up two large houses, with
the result that after fifteen years he was
£2,000 poorer than when he started." This
result would have seemed startling, if it
had not happened that the Bishop, stung
by the reproaches of his flock, once published a budget, in which he set forth,
with much precision, the details of his
expenditure. On such a system, or want
of system, as that budget revealed, the

355

only wonder is that his two thousand pounds of poverty is not ten.

" Bishops live in high places with high people, or with little people who depend upon them. They walk delicately, like Agag. They hear only one sort of conversation, and avoid bold, reckless men, as a lady veils herself from rough breezes." Let me hasten to say that these words were written by a Canon of St. Paul's, though not by one of the present Chapter. To be sure his day was not yesterday; but the testimony remains true, and " bold, reckless men," who talk of abuses and reforms, seldom have the opportunity of breathing their thoughts into episcopal ears. They can only study that wonderful paper on *Church Difficulties* which the Bishop of London wrote when he was Bishop of Stepney, and shed tears of respectful sympathy over the touching tale of harsh exaction patiently endured which " A Diocesan Bishop " contributed to that paper. They admire when they read that it cost his lordship £2,500 to settle himself

356

comfortably in his new house, and wonder if they could have done it more cheaply. They are interested to learn that the most hideous of all known costumes—the episcopal " Magpie "—costs £100, and they fancy that Mrs. Bishop could have stitched together something more comely at less cost. Hospitality to the tune of £2,000 a year rather staggers them, for their modest housekeeping assures them that a great deal of bread and mutton and table-beer can be procured for a very moderate figure. About the expenses incidental to such patriarchal appendages as wives and children—ball-gowns for the daughters and cigars for the boys—reformers do not presume to dogmatize ; and they are quite prepared to believe the " Diocesan Bishop " when he assures them that " Stables "— in the present day he would say Garages —" are almost a necessity, and in some respects a saving."

" The stair-carpets at Farnham Castle are measured by miles," wrote Bishop Thorold. " My episcopal income goes in pelargoniums," murmured Bishop Stubbs. "It takes five chaps to keep this garden in order," said a more vernacular prelate, as he surveyed his lawns. These bitter cries were not unheard.

Such hardships touched even the horny hearts of calculators and economists, and we who are Churchmen had schooled ourselves into a very proper state of mind ; we had persuaded ourselves that things are well as they are, and that "Purple, Palaces, Patronage, Profit, and Power" (as Sydney Smith enumerated them) were not only very nice for those who enjoyed them, but were, in some mysterious way never quite explained, inextricably involved in the well-being of "our pure Established Mother."

But the Bishop of London, with his engaging candour and heedless eloquence, has once again stirred the waters of controversy. If he were more worldly-wise, he would have imitated the cautious reserve of the Archbishops of Canterbury and York (both Scotsmen), who pocket much larger incomes and say nothing about them ; or he might have followed the

358

manly lead of the late Prime Minister, who said, " I draw my salary, and intend to do so," and closed the debate at that point. These public discussions of episcopal incomes disturb my peace. They remind me of John Bright's irreverent declaration :—

> If I had been a bishop, with an income of five to fifteen thousand a year, I should have had an inexhaustible source of rejoicing and merriment in the generosity, if not in the credulity, of my countrymen.

And I am apprehensive lest the spirit of that grand old iconoclast should revive in these latter days. We are told from every pulpit that, when the war is over, our national religion is to be something quite different from what we have known before. How terrible if, among other changes, it insists on a primitive episcopate, such as that of Bishop Thomas Wilson, who ruled the diocese of Sodor and Man on £300 a year ! When this comes to pass, farewell to Lambeth, with its guard-room ; and Fulham, with its pleasure-grounds ; and Farnham, with its deer-park ; and Wells, with its moated garden. We have been taught that these things endeared the Church to the toiling masses, and cheered the pallid curate in his dingy lodgings. But, if once the rash career of innovation begins, they will not long survive. Instead of them we shall see square, commodious houses of red brick, with "gravelled sweeps" and stunted laurels; and a buttony boy will discharge the functions of the stately gate-porter, and a neat damsel in a white cap will carve the episcopal beef and pour the foaming lemonade. Where, not many years ago, the Prince Bishop rolled from his castle to the parish church in a coach-and-four, his successor will trudge through the mud or scale the knife-board of the bus, carrying with his own apostolic hands the sacred appliances of Mitre or Magpie; and these will be only the outward signs of more momentous changes. The new Bishop of Exeter [1] shows tendencies in this direction, and I understand that some of his elder brethren are ready to follow in his steps.

[1] Lord William Cecil.

BISHOPS AND ECONOMY

W. F. Hook, the famous Vicar of Leeds, was neither a revolutionary nor a dreamer, and this was, seventy years ago, his remedy for the besetting weakness of the Church of England :—

We want not proud Lords, haughty spiritual Peers, to be our Bishops. Offer four thousand out of their five thousand a year for the education of the people, and call upon the more wealthy of the other clergy to do the same, and a fund is at once provided. Let Farnham Castle, and Winchester House, and Ripon Palace be sold, and we shall have funds to establish other bishoprics. Let the Church do something like this, and then the Church will live in the hearts of the people who now detest her. . . . You see, I am almost a Radical, for I do not see why our Bishops should not become as poor as Ambrose or Augustine, that they may make the people truly rich.

This letter was addressed to Samuel Wilberforce just before he became a Bishop; and the admirers of that excellent prelate will not be surprised to learn that he said in reply: "To impoverish our Bishops and sell their Palaces would only be the hopeless career of revolution."

X

CONSIDERATION

ONE of the masterpieces of Catholic literature is St. Bernard's treatise on Consideration. The Saint had been appointed by
Eugenius III to preach the Second Crusade,
which had ended in complete and apparently
hopeless failure. " Soon a murmur of wrath
and reproach was heard, which, rising in
ever-swelling volume, at last broke into
articulate utterance." Bernard was accused
and reviled as the author of the calamities
which had overtaken the Crusade. Why
had he preached it? Why had he pro-
phesied success? Why had he wrought
miracles to make men join it? The effect
of this storm was curious; not the least
what the revilers had expected, but eminently worthy of a saint. Bernard did
not recriminate; he did not even attempt

to defend his reputation for wisdom or sincerity. He let his critics rail, and calmly applied himself to his treatise on " Consideration," which he defined as " the application of the mind to the search for truth."

The particular line which his Consideration followed, though it had a strict relevance to the circumstances of the times, lies far enough off the track of our present thoughts. But the habit of Consideration —of applying the mind to the search for truth—is never out of date or out of place. It is specially useful when feelings are violently excited, and the true and eternal outline of things is obscured by temporary passions. When the war broke out, a good many people found themselves suddenly forced to undertake a function of which they had never dreamed, and, like St. Bernard, to preach a Crusade. For three years they have been preaching it " by divers portions and in divers manners." Some, like the Saint, have only incurred reproach, and, like him, they had better

363

steady their souls by serious and dispassionate thinking.

Is war a good or an evil? At any rate, we know a great deal more about it than we knew three years ago, and the modern Bernard may reply that the worst which we believed of 'it is true : that it is an unmixed and incalculable evil ; and that the man who creates it, or instigates it, or foments it, is an enemy of the human race. Is it wise to be prepared for this evil? Until the dream of a universal and simultaneous disarmament is realized, surely yes ; and here is the sole justification for navies and armies, which otherwise would be useless relics of an exploded barbarism. A nation must always be prepared for war, as an individual must be prepared for death. But is it wise to be always occupied with the thought of war, which may or may not arise within any period of time which it concerns us to consider? Bernard will answer " No." Life is not worth having at the price of an ignoble solicitude for it ; and an attitude of watchful jealousy is about the last which a great nation, conscious of its own strength, will adopt. It is better to be taken by surprise than to spend one's life in pavid apprehension of a danger which may be very far off.

Is constitutional government a failure? or, as Prince Albert put it, are representative institutions on their trial? It is one of the mischiefs of war that Englishmen should have to ask such questions; and the answer is that in war, even more conspicuously than in peace, constitutional government and representative institutions are not merely desirable, but essential. Wars may be devised by diplomatists and decreed by tyrants, but they are waged by peoples; and constitutional government is the only method, except revolution, by which a people can pass judgment on the need for war, or regulate the methods by which it is pursued. The English Constitution is a magnificent product of nationality and history, and I have no love for attempts to tinker it. But

365.

Consideration suggests that, if it needs amendment in any particular, that amendment should aim at giving the people a more direct control over the supremely important business of treaty-making and war-waging.

Is the system of government by Party played out? Here, indeed, is matter for consideration. There are moments of national crisis when the idea of Party seems absurd, and men cry out: "Away with it—let us be governed by the best and wisest, no matter what they are called." This cry was heard in August 1914, when we all agreed to think that "the best and wisest" was only another name for the Liberal Cabinet. Experience having to some extent undermined that belief, we all renewed the cry of "No Party," and agreed that a composite Cabinet was the ideal arrangement. Now, again, the Composite Cabinet is played out, and our rulers have betaken themselves to all manner of new and strange devices.

On one point, indeed, we all agree—

the absolute necessity, of winning the war. But the methods by which victory can best be assured are still the subject of lively discussion. Consideration of these facts points to the conclusion that, though we may wish to abolish Party, Party is too strong to be abolished. The spirit of freedom and the spirit of tyranny are hopelessly irreconcilable; and, though their respective followers may honestly try to coalesce, the coalition cannot long endure. Like will always tend to unite itself with like, and this union is Party.

Is it wise, in a free and self-governing nation, to enlarge the area of compulsion? All Law is indeed compulsion, and without order there can be no freedom. But the object of all reasonable men is to be governed as little as possible; and an attempt to over-govern may produce unlooked-for consequences. For example, Colonel Tufto, returning in khaki from France, may say: " A clerk who refuses to enlist—a railwayman who strikes—a munition-worker who slacks—ought to be shot." But Consideration suggests that this short and easy method would irritate, rather than terrorize, and might bring labour to an abrupt standstill precisely at the moment when its services are most vitally needed.

There is yet another topic on which St. Bernard would have urged Consideration ; and even those who will not listen to a saint may be willing to accept the same teaching from the mouth of a sage—" The beginning and, the end of what is the matter with us in these days," said Carlyle, " is that we have forgotten God." That is a defect in our arrangements, of which Committees and Blue Books take no note ; and yet, if the Divine government of the universe is not a fable, to forget it may be disastrous. The worst error which a nation can commit is not to know " the time of its visitation."